William O´Brien

'Neath silver mask´ or the cloudland of life

William O´Brien

'Neath silver mask´ or the cloudland of life

ISBN/EAN: 9783741182242

Manufactured in Europe, USA, Canada, Australia, Japa

Cover: Foto ©Andreas Hilbeck / pixelio.de

Manufactured and distributed by brebook publishing software (www.brebook.com)

William O'Brien

'Neath silver mask' or the cloudland of life

'NEATH SILVER MASK;

OR,

THE CLOUDLAND OF LIFE.

BY WILLIAM O'BRIEN.

BOSTON:
PUBLISHED BY PATRICK DONAHOE.
19 Franklin Street.
1872.

CONTENTS.

Chapter	Title	Page
CHAPTER I.	Strange Friends	1
CHAPTER II.	Light and Shadow	10
CHAPTER III.	Rolling Home	21
CHAPTER IV.	Glengarra and its Owner	35
CHAPTER V.	The Rival Candidates	44
CHAPTER VI.	Mutterings of Fate	61
CHAPTER VII.	Lord Crabshawe on the Duello	66
CHAPTER VIII.	Storm-clouds Breaking	80
CHAPTER IX.	Captain Crofts' Little Game	91
CHAPTER X.	Lucy Colthurst	100
CHAPTER XI.	Electioneering Joys	111
CHAPTER XII.	Caught in the Trap	120
CHAPTER XIII.	The Outlaws	127
CHAPTER XIV.	An Irish Election	137

CONTENTS.

CHAPTER XV.
En Suite.. 150

CHAPTER XVI.
Lord Crabshawe in Defeat............................. 161

CHAPTER XVII.
Dublin in the Olden Time 168

CHAPTER XVIII.
In the Moonlight.. 175

CHAPTER XIX.
'Twixt Life and Death................................... 179

CHAPTER XX.
Deepening Mystery...................................... 184

CHAPTER XXI.
Awaking... 192

CHAPTER XXII.
Dolce Dolore.. 197

CHAPTER XXIII.
News from Home... 204

CHAPTER XXIV.
Parting... 209

CHAPTER XXV.
The Broken Oak... 214

CHAPTER XXVI.
The Signal of Revolution............................... 219

CHAPTER XXVII.
The Death Struggle...................................... 222

CHAPTER XXVIII.
The Silver Mask... 231

CHAPTER XXIX.
Cloudland Fading... 243

CHAPTER XXX.
At Last!.. 250

'NEATH SILVER MASK;

OR,

THE CLOUDLAND OF LIFE.

CHAPTER I.

STRANGE FRIENDS.

THE sounds of footsteps and the feebling shouts of merriment retreated into the gloom. Not a living thing outstayed the murky night in the huge quadrangle of Trinity College, Dublin.

A soiltary light gleamed through the mist—a pale, flickering shadow, peeping from a window in the extreme western corner of Old Trinity. Flickering it seemed through the outward gloom, yet bright and warm the scene it illumined.

The chambers, evidently of a student not meanly circumstanced, littered with abundant testimony of wealth—walls tapestried with richest textiles, furniture lapped in the luxury of velvet, hangings gorgeous with blenditure of purple and gold, lights glowing from gilded cornices, and flashing reflections of the scene in full-length mirrors.

But confusion and recklessness everywhere. Tables strewn with half-filled glasses, furniture carelessly arranged or soiled with wine-gouts—everything betokened the ravages of the jolly set, whose tottering footsteps die away in the gloom as our tale opens.

Only two of the revellers remain—pale, exhausted, after the riotous night that had closed. Both were young men, scarcely in the bud of manhood, but in naught save age bearing the smallest similarity.

The one—the junior of his companion by a few years—was a frank, dashing youth of little over eighteen summers, with open, engaging features, handsome figure, and a voice of mellow, Munster persuasiveness. His friend was dark, handsome, perfect in face and figure, but with an indescribable something that repelled one. His keen, flashing eyes were what the world calls handsome; a pale olive tinge added interest to his white features; but not even the fascinating smile that seemed to hang continually round his lips could dispel the impression that he was more than he seemed.

Frank Inkston was, in fact, a mystery—a kind of being to whose fascination all paid homage, with the lurking suspicion that the glitter of his eye was not the flash of his soul, or the brilliance of his converse a real index to his mental workings. His early life was shrouded in impenetrable mystery. He never spoke of himself, and none dared question him. English as was his name, his features no less than his imperfect accent clearly betrayed a foreign origin; but who he really was no one divined. A couple of years he had been in Trinity, at the opening of our tale. Assiduous in his studies, and of no mean natural parts, he had gained respectable academic honors; and to the *status* thus won, he added a lavish liberality, and a semblance of gaiety, which secured him in the favor, if they did not ingratiate him in the good feeling, of the spendthrift set that at the time gave a tone so fashionably *prononce* to university society.

In strong contrast to this mysterious student was the bright-eyed boy from the hills of Tipperary, who confronted him this cheerless night. It needed not his extravagant hospitality and gay habits of life to make Charlie O'Hara the pride and favorite of Old Trinity. The bright, thoughtless boy was ever foremost in schemes of daring fun, ever candid in his friendships or his enmities, graced with every accomplishment that could fit him for the brilliant circles in which he moved, yet endowed withal, as spendthrifts rarely are, with abilities which lifted him high above his butterfly compeers in fashion or debauch.

And yet it was on this very warm-hearted southern, above all others, Inkston had fixed his regard. To every one else he was frigidly polite, or haughtily complaisant. With O'Hara he was as much of the friend and as little of the puzzle as he probably could be; and the generous-minded boy rewarded his attention with a fervid, thoughtless friendship. He loved him for the very mystery that seemed to breathe around him, pitied him even for the nameless sorrow that betimes overcast his brow and knit his olive features, yet never sought to dive into the forbidden secret. Enough for him that, to all outward seeming, Frank Inkston was a steady, faithful friend, a willing partner in his wild escapades and gay extravagances—a man, in fine, whom he ought to revere, for the all-potent reason that his affection seemed to be reciprocated.

And on this cheerless autumn night in the early years of the decade ending 1800, they sat as friends—strangely steadfast friends—and the piteous sleet whined ceaselessly at the casements, while the skeleton remnants of reverly stared blankly and coldly in the luxurious light, and a mystic rustling whisper told sadly of the spirits that were gone.

Suddenly, and as if awaking from some dreary train of thought, Frank Inkston fixed his eyes searchingly on his friend, and in a hollow, somewhat melancholy voice, asked:—

"Charlie, has the wine left you enough sobriety to talk seriously for a few moments?"

"Seriously, eh?" cried O'Hara, his fancy still soaring in a heaven of nectar and bright eyes. "Bless my soul, Frank, you have a most unhappy knack of pulling a fellow's happiness to tatters. That puckey little word 'serious,' scares all the water-sprites and wood-nymphs of imagination, just like a brace of duck-shot in a field of crows."

"Alas! though, imagination is only the sleep—earnestness the waking hours of the machine we call existence."

"What, Frank! didactic as Aristotle, by Jove! And this little moral bombshell from one head and ears in Madeira! Doesn't it strike you as slightly grotesque?"

"So are many things that are serious."

"*Exempli gratia*, the Provost dancing a Highland fling."

"Or clowns making merry in a charnel house," said Inkston, with a deeper emphasis.

"Pshaw! Frank, the subject, is getting ghastly."

"Yet I have seen you, too, serious upon occasion."

For the first time the younger man, recalled from his giddy dreams, gleamed at his companion's face, and saw pictured there in ashy, unhealthful hues, an expression he had often noted stealing over him, skeleton-like, in his gayest moments. It was one of those dim shadows of his inner soul, which floated mysteriously around the outward semblance of light-heartedness—colorless, inconstruable, yet chilling and unwholesome.

Charlie's warm heart had long settled it was the

ghost of some early grief. But whenever it came, it froze his gay humors.

"Is anything really the matter, Frank?" he asked, earnestly.

"Nothing in the world, Charlie," replied the other, a smile coming tranquilly over his olive features, "I've only succeeded in getting you in the humor I wanted. Now I feel sure you can talk as sagely as Solon."

"Ah! I see," cried O'Hara, relapsing into a lighter vein, "you've been getting up a duel on the sly. Beauteous Esmeralda—deaf mamma—indirect *billets-doux*—unappeasable big brother, and the rest of it. Well, it's the way of all flesh, Frank—bullet holes are the ordinary avenues to ladies' hearts."

"You've missed the mark, my boy," said Inkston, with a smile. "I'm not going to soil the fifteen acres, much less to come to close quarters with the meerschaum goddess. Not, though, but I'm on equally bellicose thoughts intent."

"If they be serious, then, let's have them. I always like to make one big bite of a disagreeable subject."

"You recollect not long since the night meeting in Kildare?"

"Very clearly, indeed. Such meetings don't easily escape one's memory."

"You keep in mind the brilliant promises of the Frenchman, and the fervid oratory of Wolfe Tone?"

"Ay, vividly, and the wierd solemnity with which three hundred delegates swore the sacred pact between France and Ireland!"

"Has your ardor cooled since the gathering in Kildare?"

"Well, I was a somewhat hot-headed boy at the time; but——"

"*Nous avons changé tout cela*, eh?" asked Inkston, with something between a smile and a sneer.

"Not so, by heaven!" cried the impulsive youth, warmly. "You wrong me much, Inkston, if you think inconsistency is among my failings. No: I have ceased my connection with this revolutionary movement, not because I condemn its principle, but because I distrust the narrow, halting spirit in which it is carried on. I confess my abhorrence of the bloody scenes that have been enacted in Paris in the name of liberty, and I am only too much afraid that the Irish conspiracy imitates the French hatred of broadcloth, without even the audacity of the *sans-culottes*."

"You are right, in a great measure. The first adherents of the Irish revolution were necessarily men of mean station and vulgar ambition. Now, however, it counts in its ranks some of the best and noblest blood of the country—the real bone and sinew of society, and, better than all, it counts on the speedy success of its endeavors."

"Then here's one of their most uncompromising allies!" cried O'Hara, eagerly. "God knows I have seen and felt the rapid decay of this lovely land—I have seen enough of misery and despair to convince me that nothing but a thorough uprootal of society, terrible as it may be, can renovate its jarring elements. Give me but a chance of success, and a gage that misery will not be replaced by anarchy, and thirty thousand stout Tipperary men are at the service of the revolution."

Inkston smiled calmly, satisfactorily, at the glowing enthusiasm of his friend. It was one of his occasional inscrutable smiles, that might have signified anything in the alphabet of facial telegraphy, but that could hardly be mistaken for the absorbed earnestness of the revolutionist.

"It's well, Charlie," he said. "My honor is your guarantee on both points. I am not an Irishman born, myself."

He paused, and the varying tinges of mystery crept over that face, which bore the impress, unmistakably, of a southern sun. For one moment the thought rose to O'Hara's mind—What so deep interest for the welfare of Ireland could possess this dark-faced stranger? But the next, it was dismissed as impertinent and ungenerous. Doubt was yet an undreamt-of emotion to the young enthusiast.

"I am not an Irishman by birth, myself," continued Inkston, with impassive face; "but circumstances have interested me deeply in the fate of this unfortunate land. I have lately increased my connection with the managing body of the revolutionary society, and it is on the faith of what I have seen and heard, that I assure you the hour and the signal only are wanting to plunge the country into the struggle for independence."

"Heaven grant it may not be to embitter our chalice beyond toleration!" exclaimed O'Hara, fervently.

"Impossible! success is assured."

"Well, well, it needs not success to enlist me in such a cause. I'm with you heart and soul, old boy."

"But I want you to be more than with us. You must do us a perilous, but inestimable service."

"Ah! now I can see your object."

"Precisely: I have spoken to you with an object. You must be aware that the Council of the United Irishmen here have been for a long time in negotiation with the French Directory, with the view of obtaining arms and troops. Tone, one of the alert diplomatists of the day, has carried those negotiations to so successful an issue, that the Directory have engaged, early next spring, to equip and transfer to Ireland ten thousand disciplined troops, with fifty thousand rifles for the peasantry here. General Hoche, the most illustrious and promising of the revolutionary leaders, has embarked all his energy in the project; but he is hampered by the indicision of the Directory, who seem to be wholly bent on their struggle with the Germans. Of late, Tone has observed increasing coldness in their reception of him; and he has sent word to the Dublin Directory, that it would be of vital importance that a new embassy should set out for Paris, whose accounts of the preparations and enthusiasm at home would, in all probability, bring matters to a speedy and satisfactory issue."

"And this embassy you want me to undertake?"

"Exactly! The council are of opinion that your birth, position and abilities—don't smile, Charlie—fit you pre-eminently to make the desired impression on the Frenchmen. They have, accordingly, authorized me to make you an offer of the mission."

"But why not accept it yourself, Frank?"

"I would, willingly; but being a—at least, not being a native Irishman, I would have less representative weight. Besides, I dare not set my foot in France—not yet."

"Dare not, Frank!"

"Pshaw! I don't care to go," cried Inkston, confused and annoyed at his involuntary admission.

"The mission is one that I would be delighted with," said O'Hara. "It has just the spice of adventure and excitement to take my fancy. But you know that I have set myself rather strongly on winning that Premier medal next month. Retreat would now be ignominious; for all the wits of Trinity are on the lists as my competitors."

"Ah! true," remarked his friend, with an unpleasant smile. "I will be one of your humblest rivals myself, on that occasion; so 'twould look like showing the white feather to get you out of the way. But that need make little difference. It would be impossible that anything could be done during the Winter. In the early Spring you will be quite free, and that's the exact time for doing the business."

"Then, with all my heart, I'm at your service," cried O'Hara.

"I had said as much," rejoined Inkston, again radiant with gay smiles. "Were you not a juvenile I should predict for you a niche in the capitol labelled ' *Pater Patriæ*.' But now for the practical part. Here are your credentials and instructions." He produced three little closely-sealed packets, which he handed to O'Hara. "This contains directions how to proceed at any time you may decide on going. It gives you addresses which will secure your passage to France. This contains your instructions when you get there; and here you have formal introductions to the different members of the French Directory. So now you are quite equipped for the campaign. The diplomatic part of it may with confidence be left to yourself."

"Your hand, Inkston," cried O'Hara, elated by the new and thrilling position to which he had pledged himself. "We've settled the sober part of the business—your glass to the brim, my boy! Here's—' Success to my mission!' Hip, hip, hurra!"

"Ay, ' Success to *my* mission,' " echoed Inkston, with the most delicate emphasis possible on the " my." "I drink the toast with all my heart."

CHAPTER II.

LIGHT AND SHADOW.

WE have said that few in Trinity College laid claim to equality, in point of natural ability, with Charles O'Hara, even at a time when its grand old halls were paced by men whose names are still associated with the dramatic close of Ireland's independent career. For the month succeeding that strange night interview between the friends, he put forth all that he possessed of vigor and application to second his innate powers, and what at first occurred to him as but the competition for a visionary distinction, assumed, under the influence of his new-born studiousness, all the absorbing interest and fatuous charms of a rivalry in glory. The distinction he aimed at was a gold medal, the presentation of the English Premier, offered for competition between the first honor-men of the day. Presented under circumstances especially marked, the medal provoked the jealous competition of the whole bead-roll of Irish ability, and eventually came to imply an honor equivalent to the unacademical "championship" of literary Ireland. Once having set himself to the task, O'Hara felt his interest in the result insensibly grow stronger.

Withdrawing himself imperceptibly from his ordinarily gay course of life, the impulsive youth now plunged into ascetic pursuits with as much vigor as he had previously wasted on his schemes of extravagance. Midnight saw him in wrapped intercourse with the dusty wisdom of antiquity; morning rose pale and haggard over his matin researches. The clear flush of health forsook his cheek. The sparkle of his eye became unhealthily lurid. The character of his reading seemed almost to impress itself in sickly hues upon his brow.

Almost a counterpart to those vast exertions was the assiduity with which Frank Inkston addressed himself to the self-same task. For the first time, he had come into actual rivalry with his friend; and, carefully as each strove to disguise the fact from the other, with the preparations for the great trial of strength came the bitterness inseparable from academical emulation. From whatever cause, the approach of the stuggle loosened their friendship, and infused something of coldness even into their ordinary relations.

The non-combatant dons marked easily the first symptoms of estrangement between men whose singular friendship had been to them a source of mystery and wonder. And, reviewing probabilities in their own *al fresco* style, these gowned sages came to the unanimous conclusion that the strange friendship between Inkston and O'Hara must, some morning or other, come to a question debateable only on the fifteen acres at twelve paces asunder.

At last the day of trial came, and upwards of twenty of the first minds in the country exhausted the treasures of their intellects in competition for the coveted prize. Then followed a feverish interval ere the declaration of victor. Three anxious days dragged their slow length away; and cheerily bright, in vesture of crisp December snow, opened the eventful day on which the decision of the senate was to be promulgated.

The scene in the great hall, where the ceremonial of presenting the medal was to be enacted, was truly a dazzling one—brilliant and *ecletant* as it only could be in old Dublin. The viceroy, attended by a countless train of military and official aids, uniformed with a gorgeous variety, presided over the high festival. The dais swarmed with academic magnates, and with all the hoary sages of the metropolis. The long lines of benches were thronged with the gowned undergraduates and dons of high and low degree. And to complete the charm of the *Mise en scene*, the whole fashionable world of Dublin seemed compressed into the narrow high-pitched gallery, whence the rattling of silks and the subdued peals of merriment came like presages of triumph to the dubious aspirants, whose fame the declaration of the senate was to exalt or degrade.

Seated on a retired bench beneath the gallery, O'Hara awaited with a feverish anxiety, ill-concealed, the issue of the contest. He sickened almost as he gazed round on the brilliant scene, and pictured to himself the gloom or triumph of defeat or success.

Inkston was nowhere to be seen.

The huge college bell tolled out the hour; and the proceedings commenced.

A short agonizing interview between the University authorities; then a tantalizing prolongation of the moment of suspense; and at last the Lord Chancellor arose amid a whispered anticipatory hum.

"The senate," he said, "have carefully weighed the merits of the productions submitted them by the different candidates. After long and anxious deliberation, they have unanimously awarded the palm to one manuscript. Without reflection on the other candidates, I cannot refrain from conveying the opinion of the senate, that its author is deserving of all the reward it is in our power to bestow. On examination, I have found the manuscript credited to CHARLES O'HARA,

THE CLOUDLAND OF LIFE. 13

A.B., to whom, therefore, the Premier gold medal is worthily due."

Even in that staid assembly the announcement provoked a tumult of applause. With simultaneous impulse, the whole student body rose, regardless even of the blow that had been dealt to the aspirations of many of them; and the grand old oak-lined hall rang with their lusty cheers again and again. One and all testified, in boundless terms, their joy at the success of the modest young prizeman.

Through the hazy veil of unconsciousness that stole over him, O'Hara preserved in happy memory his glorious greeting as he passed up the long aisle amid the stormy cheers of his associates, the approving smiles of the Fellows, and the eager, ill-subdued tokens of sympathy from the fair belles that crowded the gallery.

Never before had he felt the mad, pulsing throb of victory, and it came on him now with a crushing burden of joy, as if the whole world pressed on to lay its favors at his feet.

His reason almost whirled away by the furious tide of feelings that raged within his brain, he at length found himself at the foot of the dais.

Now came the presentation. The lord lieutenant rose, and, with the prettiest of speeches, placed the coveted prize in the hands of the winner.

Again the applause, waving of hats, and timid fluttering of handkerchiefs, greeted O'Hara's modest bow. This time, though, with the cessation of the applause, rose the jarring sounds of sharp verbal conflict at the principal entrance to the hall. All eyes were instantly turned to the scene whence the unseemly interruption proceeded. For a time, in the confused rush of students, it was impossible to divine the cause, and a keen, smarting pain shot across O'Hara's mind, as an unutterably sad suggestion supplied his doubts.

But a loud roar of merriment speedily dissolved his anxiety, and, to his relief, O'Hara perceived that the uproar arose from a contention between the stolid hall-porter and a low-sized, jolly-looking man, costumed as a peasant, who was in vain endeavoring to effect an entrance.

"Now, nabor, excuse me!" persisted the rustic, in most persuasive Munster tones; "the divil a lunatic out o' Bedlam would keep me on the cowld side o' the door."

"No strangers allowed to pass!" was the dogged reply; and Barebones interposed his huge *corpus* between the peasant and the door.

"Sthranger! you bitther-faced thief!" shouted the enraged frieze-coat. "You're shrinking into your boots, you ould curmudgeon! or I'd make you ate your words with a big dose of pepper! Sthranger! Bad luck to your impidence! one 'ud think 't was to the lord liftenant, or a black Saxon, you were talkin'. Stand out o' the light, instanther, Barebones, or be the 'tarnal o' war!"——

The lifted shillelagh might have emphasized the threat, but for the timely appearance of O'Hara, on whose face irrepressible amusement had replaced the ook of anxiety.

"Mick! Mick!" he cried, with difficulty averting the impending shillelagh; "for heaven's sake, don't have us up for murder!"

"Arrah, Masther Charles! it's yourself is there, is it?" shouted Mick, dismissing in a moment his angry emotions, and clutching O'Hara with a grasp of agonizing friendliness; "I knew you'd do it, my darlin' boy! Hurroo for Tipperary agin! Tipperary foriver!"

and the speaker cut a caper with surprising agility, accompanying the action by a wild whoop that completely disconcerted the august assembly.

"Mick! Mick! for heaven's sake do restrain yourself!" urged O'Hara, divided between shame and pleasure at this sudden outburst.

"Resthrain! Masther Charles!" returned Mick, "I'm as cool as well wather. Your pardon, ladies and gentlemin," he added, with an apologetic grimace directed towards the admiring bystanders. "I didn't mane to intherrupt yer jollification, only that this despicable ghost of a crature," pointing with ineffable scorn to the discomfited porter, "wanted to prevint me huggin' Masther Charles's hand, an' I own valet to himself an' his father before him! Come, byes, if it's no offince, here's three cheers for Misther O'Hara and Tipperary! Three times three, ma bouchal!"

The appeal, backed by the ringing whoop of the speaker himself, was irresistible to the impulsive students. Three deafening cheers broke from the entire body; and, before O'Hara could control his movements, he was raised on a couple of stalwarth shoulders, and borne along from the hall in tumultuous triumph, pursued by a howling train of student friends, whose lungs supplied a continuous chorus of applause, until the strange retinue reached O'Hara's chambers and triumphantly landed their victorious tenant.

A *fete* day in Trinity resembled a fourth of July celebration in New York more nearly than any other of our latter-day carnivals. Everything but amusement was ruthlessly banished; and amusement itself assumed a shape more like lunatic frenzy than quiet enjoyment. The rudimentary necessity was that everyone should be respectably drunk—a duty that most of them found to be a labor of love. Then everyone drank everyone else's health, and vowed triple-bound ties of friendship in the exhilarating atmosphere of champagne and Madeira. Some sang songs—rollicking student-choruses, with as much melody and sweetness as a regiment of organ-grinders. Others delivered abstruse orations, in which Greek roots and Irish girls, Aristophanes and Nancy Hans, Mantineia and the Phœnix Park, figured with perplexing irregularity. Then followed the really uproarious stage of the proceedings — wine-glasses smashed on fellows' heads; "meetings" innumerable arranged for the settlement of imaginary wrongs; general disposition to knock each other down for good fellowship, followed by knocker-wrenching expeditions, engagements with the college porters, and desperate efforts to maintain Old Trinity's fame amid the unsympathetic cut-throats of the Coombe.

Charlie O'Hara's entertainment to his enthusiastic friends fell short, in no particular, of the time-honored programme on such festive occasions. Inebriation, minstrelsy, oratory, pugilism—all had their turn; and the spirit of wantonness and mirth ran riot within the chambers of the successful competitor.

One shadow alone rested on the fair prospect for our hero. For a time the absence of Frank Inkston created an hiatus in the revelry. An indefinable feeling of remorse and resentment began to prey upon O'Hara's warm soul, and success seemed to have already brought its bitterness.

The feast had proceeded far, and O'Hara's increased anxiety at last attracted the attention of a huge, jolly-faced student opposite him, who, with an unsteady attempt to balance himself and the big measure of mulled claret he held in his hand, hiccuped forth:—

"Gen'lemen, 'tell you what, gen'lemen, on this auspish—auspicious 'casion—damn that punch!"—(this in anathema of a refractory jug of the native which he had just smashed into fragments)—"Gen'lemen, I was just saying when this—ahem! this—confound it! I quite forgot—I w's just going to say "——

"We won't go home until morning," suggested a watery-eyed soul on his left, amid a roar of laughter.

"Well," proceeded Danver, the first speaker, with a melancholy, broken snigger, "'tis a toast I've sincere r'spect for; but I w's going to say, on present 'casion we've met, so t' say, to drown ol' friends—or rather old foes, and what Webby calls an'mos'ties. Confound it! —can't make a speech," he blurted out at last, in hopeless confusion; "but I mean t' say, Inkston ought be here t'-night. And damme, Charlie, you ought call him out for not!"

The sentiment was received with genuine enthusiasm by the noisy roysterers around the table. "Right, Danver!" "Shoot him, Charlie!" and such like broken ejaculations rising from all portions of the room.

O'Hara was annoyed and pained at this unwelcome interlude.

"Friends," he said, amid a temporary lull in the revelry, "I beseech you not to pursue this subject. I am very far from believing that Frank Inkston has been kept by any improper motives from participating in our festivities here to-night. I am pained by his absence, but I feel sure it is not meant as an insult to me."

The words had scarcely been spoken, when, "You are right, Charlie!" came from the direction of the door, and amid an involuntary hush, Frank Inkston advanced to the chair occupied by our hero.

A deadly pallor overspread his face; his lips were bloodless, and his eyes staring vacantly; but a sickly smile hovered around his countenance.

"You will forgive me, Charlie?" he said, in his softest and most melancholy tones, gently taking O'Hara's hand. "You were correct in believing that my absence was meant to be no insult to you. But you must make allowance for disappointed hopes," he added, with a sick, weary smile. "I have been utterly prostrated with a feverish headache all day, and have only just recovered enough energy to come and add my sincere gratulations to the many your success has brought you."

The manner, no less than the tone of melancholy in which he spoke, immediately disarmed the resentment of the impulsive students, whose applause now drowned the loudness of their previous disapprobation.

Danver, who had viewed the situation with drunken stolidity, by degrees acquainted himself with the posture of affairs, and staggered up to Inkston.

"I s'pose y' heard my remark while 'go, Inkston?" he hiccuped forth; "I said you 're infernal scoundrel. It's all right now. Beg par'n, 'n all that, Inkston. The devil's not so bad as he's painted; or rather——. Confound it! Inkston, I meant make 'n apology, you know. How'v'r, I don't mind giving you a shot at me in the morning. Here, Archie!" he cried to one of his neighbors, "you make that all right! Choice weap'ns yours, Inkston, ol' boy?"

"Many thanks, my dear fellow," returned Inkston, with a smile; "I won't avail myself of your generosity this time, and accept of your apology *nolens volens*. A toast, boys!" he added, raising a foaming goblet to his lips. "Here's to Charlie O'Hara, and confusion to his foes! Hip, hip, hurra!"

The glasses were drained, the hurra rang through the chamber, and amid a scene of boisterous gaiety the feast went merrily on.

THE CLOUDLAND OF LIFE. 19

* * * * * * * *

Fatigued and exhausted, Frank Inkston reached his rooms that night. The buoyancy of an hour since had abandoned him, and in its place glared a weird, mysterious passion. The clouds had again closed over his strange existence.

Flinging his cap impatiently to a far corner of the room, he called for his servant, James.

Immediately a lean, raw-head-and-bloody-bones figure, like the ghost of a departed sexton, glided into the room.

"Called, sah?" he timidly inquired.

"Yes. Get me a light; and then see that no one disturbs me for the night."

"Yes, sah," and James again skated out of the room, to return with the required light, after arranging which he stole away with the noiselessness of a mouse.

For awhile his master leaned wearily against his escritoire, his face buried in his white hands, and a suppressed groan now and again testifying to the bitterness of his thoughts.

Then he rose abruptly, and turned the key of the escritoire. Cautiously glancing around, he touched a spring. A small-sized drawer flew open, and disclosed a carefully sealed packet.

Inkston impatiently broke the seals, and produced from the folds of the packet two miniature portraits. He pressed them eagerly, almost madly, to his lips. There was reverence, love—absorbing love—in the devouring wildness of his glance. He seemed to feed on the faces enshrined in those little pictures.

Gradually the fire in his eye assumed an unearthly brilliancy. His pale face was wrought into black by the fierce tumult of passion.

"*O ciel!*" at last he cried in an agony of thought, and he sank into a chair, with his head resting on his white hand.

And the portraits dropped from his grasp.

They contained the heads of a man and a woman—the latter of surpassing beauty, the former of a harder and rather repulsive stamp. Both bore the impress of high rank, and both betrayed, in the contour and color of their features, a continental origin.

The flickering taper burnt slowly away, and still Inkston remained buried in his passionate reverie. There was something terrible in his look, something horrible in the glare of his coal-black eye.

Suddenly the silence was broken by the little clock on the mantel as it told out the passing hour. Inkston started to his feet, and lifting the portraits, clutched them firmly in his grasp.

And he murmured in passionate accents the horrid thoughts that seared his brain—muttered them, though, in a foreign tongue, and in strange, broken syllables:

"One other coal to the furnace of my thoughts," were his last words, as he sank unconsciously into his chair, and the gray light of morning, stealing in through the windows and shrouding the deathly flicker of the taper, disturbed the reverie of the MYSTERIOUS STUDENT.

CHAPTER III.

ROLLING HOME.

A FEW days after his carrying off the great Premier prize in Trinity, O'Hara left Dublin to return home during the Christmas holidays, then near at hand. He was accompanied by his friend, Frank Inkston, whom he desired to make the acquaintance of those at home.

The morning was a keen December one—the sky suffused with snow-clouds, and the atmosphere steeped in biting winds—as our friends rattled away on the Kilkenny road, in one of those lumbering, choky caravans, known in the parlance of the time as a "postchaise." The conveyance was drawn by two dissipated-looking steeds, with inconvenient bones and famine-stricken flanks. "Like master, like man," the driver was a lank, out-at-elbow savage, whose sole remarkable features seemed to be a blazing eye and a thirsty-looking lip. Ragged as were all the component parts of the team, they yet seemed to work in marvellous unison—chaise, horses and driver spinning along with a precarious speed, that would rather befit a Galway steeple-chase course than that dignified belt of highway known as the king's mail-coach road.

O'Hara and his friend were stowed away inside, and beguiled, as best they might, the tedium of the endless drive. The luggage occupied the roof of the coach, and on the box-seat, with the driver, were Mick Hoolohan, our hero's attendant, and "James," the taciturn retainer of Frank Inkston. As Mick's *debut* left us no opportunity for minute description, we may as well sketch him in brief.

He was one of those purely Irish peasants of which Tipperary was so prolific in the latter part of the last century. Fun and adoration of Ireland were the ruling ingredients of his character. His leanings were wholly aristocratic, without being flunkeyish. Tradition had assigned the Hoolohans an honored place in the service of the O'Hara's from time immemorial, and Mick accepted the position with unreasoning fidelity. Whether a head was to be broken, a bailiff soused, or a girl eloped with, Mick was an ardent volunteer, provided it was in the service of an O'Hara. He would hew out the way to heaven for one of the beloved race; or follow his master to the courts of Hades with equal alacrity. We have little doubt that, did the inclination of the O'Hara family tend that way, he would willingly immure himself in a Dominican friary; but, failing such a pious *penchant* on their part, Mick felt himself at liberty to revel at will in the world of fun and frolic his genial spirits ever created around him. There was, nevertheless, beneath his brimming jollity, an undercurrent of sincerity and affection, which, like silver-chinks in the Andes, shone all the more brilliantly because of its *farouche* setting.

In striking contrast with this merry Irishman was the morose and silent James. Beyond his Christian name, James had never disclosed a single clue to his identity. He had come to Trinity College with Frank Inkston, but, if the master was reticent, the servant was wholly tongue-tied; and even voluble Mick Hoolohan had failed to extract from him one disclosure to allay the curiosity respecting his early life. His face favored the mystery, for it was utterly meaningless—a yellow piece of parchment, patched with the facial protuberances. He never betrayed emotion, either of joy or of sorrow, save on rarest occasions; and had his words been gold nuggets he could not hoard them with more miserly care. He was, in short, one of those men so often to be met with in the world, who might pass unnoticed, but that they provoke the inquiry, what in the world they want there.

Freighted with such occupants, the lumbering old chaise dashed along towards its destination in Tipperary. As they proceeded, the omens of the morning bore fruit. The clouds let down their feathery burden in softest sheaves. The snow blinded the whole atmosphere, and whitened every object with its virgin cloak. The chaise soon partook of the general whitewashing. The driver's ragged habiliments were saturated with the liquid element—but the driver had an unfailing antidote for external moisture in the nameless black bottle he occasionally produced; and the effect was that in proportion to the inclemency of the weather, Jehu's animal spirits were tremendously on the increase. Mick Hoolohan was too much of an Irishman to be disconcerted by the vagaries of the weather; but was enough of one to hold sympathetic communion with the jarvey over the black bottle. As for James, he remained in dignified isolation, peering out from his snuggery of furs with impressive stare on the snowy wild.

Within, Charlie O'Hara chatted away the tedious hours with numberless plans for making his friend enjoy the visit, and countless little tales of his friends at home. Frank Inkston listened with even more than ordinary attention, and at least simulated the liveliest interest in every detail connected with O'Hara's family.

He was graver than usual, though, and his gayest allusions to the jolly time he intended to have at Glengarra were dashed with discomfort and melancholy.

But his joyous companion was not to be damped by such dismal forebodings. The prospect of a return home, with the whole train of lovely associations it called up, sharpened his imagination, and precipitated him into glowing pictures of Glengarra and its denizens.

"And the girls, my dear boy," he ran on, in warm panegyric on Tipperary, "they're something gorgeous. None of your milk-and-water beauties of the Royal, with more bella-donna than fun in their eyes—*morbleu!* though, we must beg their pardons, for we've often sworn it was the light of love. But Tipperary girls, my boy, are the genuine gold—diamond eyes, pearly teeth, rosy lips, and *such* feet! By Jupiter, Frank, you must be a Minerva in plain clothes, if you leave Tipperary unsmitten. I've set them all on tiptoe, too, to see what sort you are. I don't boast much of my style of composition, but I've written to Milly such a gushing picture of the handsome young student, with the raven-black hair, and the pale, thoughtful face, as will, I fancy, make half the girls in the barony in love with you before they see you at all. *Facilis est descensus Averni;* take care, my dear boy, you don't get swallowed up one of those mornings in the matrimonial pit."

While the unreflective boy ran on, his words seemed as daggers to Frank Inkston. Cloud chased cloud over his closely-knit brow, and a look of unspeakable agony settled on his face.

At length O'Hara noted the change.

"Why, you are sick, Frank," he cried, with the deepest concern. "Surely, I have not pained you."

"Oh! no, no!" cried Inkston, shaking off with a desperate effort his pressing grief, and seizing O'Hara's hand in a sudden and almost mad paroxysm of affection. "No, Charlie, *you* have never pained me."

"*Who* has, then? For heaven's sake, Frank, tell me. There is some fearful grief weighing you down. Often and often I have noticed it. Tell it to me, Frank, and I may be of use to you. Surely, I am enough your friend to merit your confidence."

The generous appeal only lashed his companion into a wilder frenzy.

"Yes, yes, Charlie!" he cried, "you are my friend. Oh! you are *too* true a friend," and O'Hara's hand fell from his grasp, while a tear of distilled agony glittered in his flashing eye.

"Then why not trust me, Frank?"

"I cannot, I cannot! *Not now*," was the terribly earnest reply.

"*Cannot*, Frank? Oh! think, my dear fellow. This is all very, very strange to me; but I feel I can relieve you, if you only confide in me."

He looked up pleadingly into his companion's face; but started back affrighted at the spectacle.

Were all the furies tearing for mastery in his countetance, they could not more desolate it. The workings of that face were something dreadful to see. The ashy whiteness of passion gathered over it. For a moment he seemed as if he would start up and embrace the generous-souled boy that confronted him. Another moment, and the giant strength of his resolution had mastered the impulse. The glassy tear that stood in his eye was parched up; the pale olive returned to his face, and something like a ghastly smile lingered round him, as he cried:

"Pshaw! Charlie, I have been an awful fool, to talk of confidences and all that, when I had really nothing to confide. These are but humors of mine—shadows, perhaps, of early life. But you'll forgive me now, Charlie—now that it's all over?"

"Very well, Frank," was the somewhat sad response. "If there was anything to annoy you, I should be glad to give you any consolation in my power. But, now you say there is not, why, I would be the last in the world to ask you an impertinent question."

"Thanks, thanks!" said Inkston, cordially shaking his hand. "One thing more, though; you believe I *feel* as a friend?"

"Why, what a strange question!" cried O'Hara, in amazement.

"Of course it *is* strange, and stupid," said the other, as if repenting of his remark. "One stupidity betrays me into another. But let us have no more about it, Charlie. How goes our journey?" and the speaker resumed his old *nonchalant* tone as he leaned out of the window.

"Why, bless me!" he cried, suddenly starting back, "we're positively flying over this road. See! almost a mile a minute; and how the coach *does* rock. Oh! this will never do; we'll be smashed to pieces in a trice."

"And confound me," chimed in O'Hara, who had also jumped to the window—"there's that fellow of mine lashing the unfortunate horses as if they were but trotting!"

It was, indeed, high time for them to pay attention to the speed at which they were rattling along the uneven road. His devotions to the black bottle had at length prostrated the driver, who dropped the reins with a drunken "hurra," and resigned himself contentedly to the benign influence that was upon him. What had floored the driver, only strenghened the nerves and maddened the spirits of Mick Hoolohan. Having first bundled the defunct jarvey into a convenient vacuity among the trunks on the roof, he assumed the "ribbons" himself, and used them, too, with right good will.

"M'agragal," he muttered, in confidential colloquy with the nags, "'twas I could handle the whip in my day, an' never fear it but I'm able to do a little that way yet. Come, we ought to be near Tipperary now, ye bastes, an' call me Davy but I'll have ye fresh an' fastin' at Glingarra gate before ye're two hours oulder. Whillilew!"

And with a crack of the whip off went the team. Tickled by the application of "the silk," the horses broke first into a gallop, and then into a wild, maddened career. With blazing eyes and strained limbs the creatures seemed to partake of the daring spirit of the driver, and dashed away at a speed that a thorough-bred racer would have shrunk from.

Delighted immensely at this improvement in the pace, Mick humored the horses to the top of their bent. Fast as they went, Mick wanted them to go faster. "Tipperary speed!" he shouted, with glowing cheeks, as he flung the reins to the leader, and hedge, ditch, and tree flew past in dizzy succession, while the unwieldy old chaise rocked from side to side, and spun madly along like an inebriated steeplechaser.

For a time the imperturbable James witnessed the alarming change with stoical fortitude; but his nerves at last gave way before the utterly reckless pace they were falling into, and with might and main he bellowed out to Hoolohan to stop.

The alarm of poor James served only as an incentive to Mick's jocularity. Slash! came the whip again on the backs of the unfortunate horses, and forward they bounded, until the snow began to beat their faces like fragments of a stone wall.

It was at this very interesting juncture of affairs that Frank Inkston's attention was so accidentally drawn to the break-neck rapidity with which they were traversing the ground.

But all efforts were now in vain to stay their fearful course. In vain O'Hara in turn swore at, commanded, and implored of Mick to pull up. In vain he bellowed in his ear the imminent certainty of destruction if he proceeded.

With blazing eye and glowing cheek, he yelled out his encouragements to the horses, and whooped out his laughing praise over the pace they had attained.

The short day had already closed, and darkness was gathering all around; yet onward Mick held his course through the blinding snow.

But it could not last. Just at the moment that O'Hara was contemplating jumping from the chaise to chastise the refractory driver—smash! went coach, horses, and all, into a deep dyke by the roadside, and amid a stifled cry and a thundering crash the entire machine collapsed.

Our hero recovered from a period of blissful unconsciousness to find himself comfortably jammed in among the *débris* of the coach. Inkston was standing over him endeavoring to disengage him, and a few country people who had collected with lanterns were muttering sundry wishes for his *post mortem* felicity around him. Having with ease extricated himself, O'Hara could not forbear a hearty laugh at the ridiculous aspect of the *mise en scene*—the horror-stricken piety of the rustics, the lamentable jelly into which the chaise had been pounded, shafts, axles, and wheels strewn about in every direction, and the unfortunate horses galloping away in the distance, rejoicing in their unwonted freedom.

A little examination satisfied him that he had not himself sustained any very serious results from the catastrophe. Inkston was quite unharmed. Two bodies flung to the far end of the road in the concussion were found to be those of James and the driver, the former of whom, when he awoke, viewed the situation with lofty contempt, while the latter slept on in happy unconsciousness of his ruined hopes and chaise.

Mick Hoolohan was standing in philosophic meditation over the consequences of his freak.

"Well, bad scran to thim bastes, anyhow," he at last muttered, apostrophizing the retreating cattle. "*Why the divel did they go so fast whin they weren't able to hould ?* 'Twas a wondher they didn't sind us all to ould Nick 'idout judge or jury."

This dubious remark turned the reproof on O'Hara's lips to an irrepressible smile.

"Mick, this is a most unpardonable night's work," was his feeble remonstrance.

"Begor, you may say that, Masther Charles. I'll bate the blaguards black and blue whin I ketch 'em. Howsimever, we must be a little considberate in regard to dumb bastes, that doesn't know how to go along a straight road dacently 'idout falling into a dyke."

The philosophy was conclusive, and our hero looked around cheerfully to see what could be done under the circumstances.

A little inquiry from the country people satisfied him that they had arrived within four or five miles of Clonmel, at a short distance from which Glengarra was situated. So far they were fortunate, and, having arranged with Mick the composition for the smashed chaise and the broken bones of its driver, O'Hara was reconciling himself to a walk home, when the sound of wheels were heard in the darkness, and in a minute or two after a rumbling dogcart was pulled up near where they were standing, while a jolly voice from the vehicle sang out:

"Hallo, there! what's up? By my oath, I believe 'tis celebrating High Mass ye are, or holding a Whiteboy meeting!"

"Jack Colthurst's voice among a thousand!" cried O'Hara, springing to the side of the car.

"The same, on my mother's authority," said the individual in the dogcart, stooping to scan the speaker. "The devil! why you can't be—and yet that is—Charlie O'Hara, how the devil are you?" and Jack Colthurst, at length satisfied of our hero's identity, leaped lightly from the cart, and clutched him in a cyclopean grasp.

"In the name of all that is wonderful," he said, after the first greetings had been interchanged, "what brings you here at such a time or in such a way? 'Tis confounded well for you I don't hold a commission in the 'yeos,' or I wouldn't know what to think of your loyalty. But this is Mick Hoolohan, and this——"

"A particular friend of mine, Mr. Inkston—Captain Colthurst. One of my college chums, Jack. I am bringing him down to see Tipperary."

"Faith, then, you're likely to see enough of it within the next week or two, Mr. Inkston," said the captain. "We'll have roaring fun at the election. You didn't hear of it, Charlie? But never mind; I'll tell you all about it by-and-by. Meanwhile, what the reprobate has happened you?"

O'Hara briefly explained to him the circumstances of their disaster.

"Pheugh! if that be all," he said, "I'm just going round by Glengarra myself, and I'll drop you there with a heart and a half, in time to get reasonably inebriated before bedtime."

Our hero's difficulty was thus pleasantly smoothed away. Leaving Mick to his own ingenuity to get rid of the chaise, and take care of James and the driver, O'Hara and Inkston joined the captain in the drag, which rattled away towards Clonmel at a merry jogging pace.

The night continued to spread its snowy, blustering

horrors around, but the journey passed pleasantly enough for the friends, who speedily glided into an animated resumé of their several doings since last they met.

Captain Colthurst was a man entirely after O'Hara's own fashion—young, thoughtless, and jovial to the very innermost of his soul; and the reminiscences they raked up of their mutual good doings were seasoned with a fund of anecdote and an unintermittent flow of humor that rendered them a peculiarly interesting entertainment for Frank Inkston, who himself scarcely interfered by a word in their communings.

"But about this election you were speaking of," suggested O'Hara, after they had run over the whole chapter of accidents by flood, field or woman.

"Upon my soul, I was near forgetting all about it, Charlie—like the omadhawn that went to pay his rounds at the Holy Well, and fell in love with the girl he found there, instead. But you'd never guess what an interest I ought to have in this same election."

"Perhaps you're going to be whisky-distributor-in-chief," suggested O'Hara.

"Something higher still, my friend. I'm THE POPULAR CANDIDATE."

"The devil you are!" was his friend's involuntary ejaculation.

"Not till I become an Irish M. P., if you please," said the captain blandly; "one must graduate in College Green to gain satanic honors. But in all seriousness, Charlie—and I *can* be serious at times, as a certain wizened old balliff once candidly admitted when I pitched him out of the window—in all seriousness, I'm fairly ' up for the county.' "

"But I've not heard a word about it. I didn't even hear there was a vacancy."

"I'll put the whole thing in a nutshell for you. Old

Crabshawe died the other day; young Crabshawe wants to succeed him in the representation of Tipperary. Jack Colthurst wants him *not—ergo*, young Crabshawe and Jack Colthurst will have to fight it out. There's the entire *quod erat demonstrandum* in fewer words than many men would use to say 'How d'ye do?' But now, to descend from the misty region of generalization—as the old lord chancellor says on state occasions—I have got very earnest about this business. If 'twere only a thing personally between Crabshawe and myself I wouldn't waste a thought on it, for it could be amicably settled to the tune of 'one, two, three!' But you see it has been made a devilish big affair. Grattan says the honor of the county is involved in the contest, and when I knew Grattan long ago he was generally right. Fact is, old Crabshawe was the bitterest scoundrel that ever cleared an estate, or bred bum-bailiffs by the hundred. He was, besides, in Parliament a dreadful stickler for everything English; but the old villain was so powerful among all the big fellows in Tipperary, that you might as well throw stones at the rock of Cashel as say 'boo!' to him at an election. The son is very much more stupid; but that is the only point in which he approaches virtue nearer than his father. Now, Grattan says such fellows must be swept out of the way, or some day or other the whole Irish people will be bundled into perdition. I believe it; for my own experience is, we're approaching the tropical regions at a gallop every day. Well, the short and the long of it is, Grattan knows me pretty well, and he has induced me to take up the cudgels against this scented piece of nobility."

"But surely, Jack," said O'Hara, "you've considered the chances. Lord Crabshawe has the entire power of the landlords at his command, and we all know that few care to stir against them."

"That's exactly why I've determined to go on," was

the sedate reply. "I'm a bit of a landlord myself—that is, barring mortgages innumerable—and I don't care if all the landlords in creation were to the fore, I'd maintain that every man has a right to choose whom he pleases. I'll take up that stand during the election; and, by the powers, I'll see that every man has a chance of saying whether I'm right or no. 'Twill be a desperate tug, Charlie. Every tenant in the county has been warned to give me the cold shoulder; but everywhere I've gone, thousands of fine fellows rushed cheerfully to me, and by Jupiter! I would be betraying them and myself if I did not run it out to the winning-post. I was canvassing all day to-day out near Thurles, made just thirty-four speeches, shook some five thousand hands, ate a couple of hundred dinners, drank whiskey enough to float a three-decker, and, without egotism, I must say, acquitted myself to satisfaction in the character of popular candidate. The people are mad in the cause, my boy, and 'tis really worth fighting for. If we're beaten, why, I'll take right good care to pick a quarrel with a couple of hundred landlords, and rid the country of an entire plague of locusts."

O'Hara smiled at the rough-drawn picture, and at the big, jovial friend who drew it.

"Well, Jack Colthurst," he said, "now you've fairly embarked in the thing, here's one that will follow you to the death."

"Thanks, thanks, old fellow," said Colthurst, warmly grasping his friend's hand. "I knew I might count on you, and you are really a host in yourself, for devil a more popular fellow from the Keeper to Slivenamon. But there is one difficulty, Charlie—I fear your father will be against us; Crabshawe and himself were fast friends, and besides, you know he hates the popular party in parliament as the devil does holy water."

"Ah! true." reflected O'Hara, sadly, "I never thought of that. He will be against us, and will be a vehement opponent, too."

"Then I'll hold you released, old boy," cried the captain, "I only ask your neutrality."

"Not so," said O'Hara warmly. "I have learned to think for myself, and it would be but a poor exemplification of my doctrine if I were to be led away against principles, country and friend by the whim of my father. I am sorry, exceedingly sorry, for the necessity, but now that it has arisen I can see that your cause is a glorious one, and I'm pledged to it at any risk. Besides, my poor father is growing old now, and I scarcely think he will care to embroil himself in an election struggle at his time of life. I feel certain I can manage to make him neutral, at any rate."

"And Milly has promised, also, to do what she can with him," added Colthurst; "so that—pardon me—he must be the most heartless curmudgeon from this to himself if he be deaf to such sweet entreaty. But, hallo! that's like your front gate there. Good-bye, Charlie—I won't go up to the house to-night. I might spoil my chances. Promise me you will give us a call—say to-morrow night. Lucy will be dying to see you."

"With pleasure, my dear friend," said O'Hara, as he alighted from the car. "Meanwhile, kindest remembrances to Miss Lucy, and success to your campaign for Tipperary."

"All right, old boy. Good-bye, Mr. Inkston. We'll show you a little of Tipperary before you leave, I warrant," and with a last warm-hearted "good night" the captain and his team disappeared in the gloom, and Frank Inkston and our hero turned into the great avenue that led to Glengarra House.

CHAPTER IV

GLENGARRA AND ITS OWNER.

GLENGARRA House, the residence of the O'Haras from time immemorial, was almost old and heterogeneous enough to tell its own history. Composite would be an inadequate term to convey any idea of the varied elements of a building—the castellated battlements of the old Norman times, the frailer turrets of latter days, and the handsome colonnades and virgin masonry of eighteenth century construction. The main body of the buildings, clothed with ivy, or frowning with dark rubble masonry, conveyed the idea of a strong fortified place—an idea strengthened by the portholed-turrets and grass-grown fosse. Such had originally been its mission; but more peaceful ages had gradually decayed the warlike paraphernalia of Glengarra. Time after time innovations of a modern order had supplanted the old feudal fortifications, until, at the period of our story, the inhabited parts give it more the aspect of a handsome modern mansion. It was still, however, a rambling, disjoined sort of place, with a hoary old turret peeping out in one corner, and a slice of heavy ivied battlement struggling amid a crowd of cut-stone buildings in another. The board plateau fronting the main entrance formed a spacious carriage sweep, while on every side of the house stretched away to the distant mountains a noble extent of wooded park, rich in every art-feature that could heighten the *picturesquerie* of nature. The entire landscape, the majestic old mansion, the venerable trees, the boundless lawn, all assured one of an ancient and honored house; yet neglect and decay were stamped upon all. The older parts of the mansion were tottering in many places; the grass crept in upon the gravelled drive; everything around was unkept and rude; parterres of what had once been flowers were overgrown with rank weeds; the hand of the destroyer was visible in the mangled trees and torn underwood; horses and cattle mingled with the deer in the park; while over all hung a melancholy stillness, made more painful by the rude shriek of the crows among the ivy, and the distant murmur of waters in the valley.

As is invariably the case, the appearance of Glengarra was in keeping with the character of its master. At the period of our tale, the head of the O'Hara family was our hero's father, Mr. Redmond O'Hara, a man in every respect singular, and at variance with his fellows. Rumor had it, that his youth was spent amid scenes of debauchery and excitement seldom surpassed. His father had been one of the staunchest friends of the unfortunate King James during his disastrous campaign in Ireland. In early youth, Redmond had been fascinated by the romantic struggles of the "Blackbird;" and when Sarsfield's brigade was winning laurels imperishable on the battlefields of the continent, he sought and obtained his father's consent to cross over to France. His engaging manners and captivating bravery soon gained him high repute at the court of the dethroned monarch; and between the brilliant salons of King Louis' gorgeous court and the more modest *réunions* at St. Germains, the handsome young Irishman shortly became a prominent figure in French society. He crossed over to Scotland with the elder and younger Pretenders, during the famous rebellions of '15 and '45, and won increased renown during those romantic episodes.

Suddenly, while his credit at the French court seemed highest, and his prospects in the future seemed to be opening into a dazzling vista, Redmond O'Hara quitted France secretly, easily obtained King George's pardon and a confirmation of his estates, and passed back to his home in Tipperary a strangely altered man. The vigor and energy of his manhood remained; but all its bright promise seemed to be blasted. The fascinating manners that had graced him in society disappeared; a deep, sullen passion, in whose mystery he seemed to be perpetually brooding, replaced the bright smile and buoyant heart of younger days. The neighboring gentry had almost forgotten him during his absence; and he studiously avoided renewing the connection. Though the master of almost boundless estates, he secluded himself diligently from the world; his moroseness degenerated into tyranny, and he was hated by his tenantry; but, on the rare occasions when he came in contact with his social equals, he was still the gentleman in conventional courtesy, though never the friend in its warmer relations.

A couple of years after his return he married a fair young wife, who bore him two children; but she soon after died, people whispered from a broken heart. The care that thus devolved upon him of his youthful offspring softened somewhat the almost savage rudeness into which he was sinking. The loveliest of lovely daughters and a rosy-cheeked blooming boy soon cheated the frown from his brow, and bent somewhat the iron stubbornness of his grief. He loved them both with absorbing affection, and his love for them by degrees drew him into kindlier relations with his neighbors.

But the shadow was never completely effaced from his brow.

He had by the time we write of advanced far in the winter of his age; the frown on his forehead had settled into deep-ploughed furrows, and his hair was seamed with dark gray threads. But the giant figure had lost nothing of its majestic erectness, his eye could still blaze with the olden fierceness, his voice was as commanding and stern as ever. His vast estates had fallan into utter confusion; rents were irregularly paid, but occasionally exacted with arbitrary cruelty; the mansion and grounds were totally neglected; and the old man persistently clung to the reticence and moodiness for which he had been remarked on his return from the continent. Naturally, such a man was in no great favor with the humbler classes, who hated and feared him heartily; while he, on his side, maintained a hauteur and contempt for every democratic invasion that widened the gulf between himself and his tenants.

His only connecting links with the outer world were his children—Charles O'Hara, whose acquaintance we have made, and Emily O'Hara, whom it is full time we should introduce to the reader.

In most vivid contrast with her father was this loveliest specimen of an Irish beauty. As much as he was gloomy, harsh, and cruel, Milly was gay, lightsome, and considerate. The gloom that overshadowed his life cast not a reflection on her joyous spirit. The society which he shunned with besetting zeal, she shone in as in a congenial world. And little wonder that Milly O'Hara did not copy the hermit-like seclusion of her father, for few more beauteous gems adorned this commonplace world. Her beauty was not the cold perfection of a Madonna—it was the laughing loveliness of a light-hearted child of nature; her flowing black hair knew no conventional restraint; her flashing black eyes roamed at will; her ripe red lips never harbored a sigh; she lived in an atmosphere of smiles and fun —a gay, lovely creature, without a thought, save to make every one happy. The death of her mother while she was yet an infant removed from her those womanly influences that mould other girls so imperceptibly. Her inclinations tended further to give her a contempt for the restraints of society; and she grew up in a wild beauty that added an irresistible attraction to her natural charms. She was at this time just eighteen years old, in the full peachy bloom of girlhood, and, notwithstanding some eccentricities inseparable from her mode of rearing, was gifted with a matchless grace which gave attraction to her maddest gaieties, and rendered her one of the most loveable girls in Tipperary. By her father she was passionately cherished; by the peasantry, absolutely adored; and by every member of the society in which she moved, courted with the most assiduous attentions. She entered, besides, into all the amusements of the people and the gentry; attended a hurling-match one day, rode to cover the next; at one time breaking hearts and scattering malicious smiles in some gilded drawing-room; at another, carrying life and beauty among the cabins of the poor.

Yet Milly O'Hara was careless to a degree. She had rather see a thorough-bred cared for in the stables than a flower-bed trimmed in the garden; and was indifferent if the weeds grew in the avenue so that the laugh and the shout went up from the green. Thus, between the careless daughter and the sullen father, Glengarra waxed gradually shabbier, and mansion and grounds were fast hastening to decay.

When Charles O'Hara and his friend arrived at Glengarra House that blustering wintry night, they found the inhabitants of the old mansion in eager expectation of their coming. The old man had for once shaken off his inveterate fits of gloom to do fitting honor to the friend of a son whom he clung to with passionate, though undemonstrative affection. Miss Emily was beaming with delight, eager to kiss poor dear Charlie after the many weary months he had been away from her and Glengarra, and eager, too, mayhap—as what girl would not be?—to see what sort of man was the mysterious, handsome student, whom Charlie's letters had surrounded with a halo of interest.

And she *did* kiss Charlie—with no studied grace, either, but with her white hand entwining his neck in fondest embrace, and her ripe, rosy lips bathing his with perfumed kisses.

And she tripped up to his friend with an evident determination to repeat the process. But no! she almost started as she looked into that face, so haggardly fascinating—that eye flashing so unquiet a soul—and even *her* enthusiasm was cooled into a rather constrained greeting.

Mr. O'Hara welcomed his visitor with polished courtesy, and did all the honors of his house with the *haute politesse* of the old cavaliers. Charlie was surprised and pleased at this semblance of gayety—or, rather, of that shadow of a smile that could alone find place on his stern visage.

"This old place has been falling into decay very much lately, Mr. Inkston," he said, with the slightest tinge of sadness in his tone. "I am not myself a great adept in arboriculture, and the park has been running wild with unthinned timber. Then, the house is somewhat old-fashioned, and we all live so quietly that we cannot promise you many of the enjoyments you might look for in the house of an Irish gentleman."

"Oh! pardon, papa," interrupted Milly, somewhat piqued at the depreciation of the ancestral domains; "Glengarra is scarcely so dark a place as you paint it. Papa lives so quietly himself, Mr. Inkston, that he imagines all the world should shut themselves up in a dusty old library, and pass life amid a nest of cobwebs."

"I fancy *you* have not given much latitude to doctrines so heterodox," said Inkston, with an admiring glance at the rich rosy cheeks of the speaker.

"No, indeed, I don't lay any claim in the world to a martyr's crown. I know a good deal of what they do about here, and, I can assure you, there is no more stirring place in the world. Between fox-hunting, steeple-chasing, duelling, and shooting, we contrive to pass most merry existences."

"Tipperary enjoys a special reputation for the last species of amusement," said Inkston.

"Well, yes. The upper classes here are at a small disadvantage—for, along with shooting one another, landlords must occasionally submit to be shot at by vulgar outsiders—which, of course, is very provoking; only that the peasantry are so discriminating, they seldom shoot any that don't deserve it."

"Milly, you are an incorrigible socialist," said her father, in a tone of subdued displeasure.

"Yes, Miss O'Hara seems to have drawn inspiration from France," put in Inkston, in a voice of almost startling clearness.

For the first time his eyes met those of his host, in a searching and fascinated glance. What secret power was in those eyes that caused that stern old man almost to jump from his seat? What fatal charm had the words that drew that deadly pallor on the old man's cheek?

Who could tell? for, the instant after, Inkston was his old impassive self; and Mr. O'Hara recovered the self-possession so strangely shaken by this interchange of glances.

But the old man was, beyond doubt, smitten with the strange fascination—half voluntary, half compulsory—of that mysterious presence. Henceforth, he was more than the courteous host—he took a deep, absorbing interest in his guest.

"Well, I don't understand much of the ill things they say of France," said Milly, unconscious of this mute episode. "They say the French have got rid of their king—well, I suppose they have not done so without reason. But I think 't is very wicked of them to go hanging the aristocracy—that is, if they're like the aristocracy here; for we really have some of the finest and the jolliest fellows in the world among our upper classes. Now, there's Jack Colthurst, for instance—Captain Colthurst, I mean."

"Oh! by-the-by, father," said Charlie, rejoiced at the opportunity, "I suppose you've heard that Captain Colthurst is going to contest the county."

"And to make a fool of himself," interrupted his father, with acrimonious sharpness.

"Well, I don't know that," persisted O'Hara, "I confess I see every prospect of success; and, even in the event of defeat, Jack Colthurst is not the man to make a fool of himself."

"That's just what I've been impressing on him for the last two days," said Milly, in her most coaxing accents. "Indeed, papa, you are too obstinate. Just fancy taking up a senseless booby like Lord Crabshawe, instead of big, jolly Jack Colthurst, that every one in the world loves." The lovely girl almost blushed at the last candid declaration.

"Captain Colthurst is fortunate in securing advocates so irresistible," observed Inkston, rather emphatically.

"Nevertheless," said Mr. O'Hara, all his courtesy

freezing into severity, "Captain Colthurst's advocates are not successful ones. The fact is, Captain Colthurst is a gentleman whose only recommendation seems to me the love of mischief. He has introduced his infernal stupid-headed doctrines about liberty, and equality, and all that, here, and wants to stir up the unfortunate people to repeat the performances of their Parisian brothers. But he shall find his mistake. In me, at any rate, he will find an uncompromising enemy. Sir, I have seen and known that *vieille noblesse* whom the base scum of Paris are now putting to the guillotine by scores, and "—— He stopped abruptly, and as if pained that his warmth had led him into forbidden paths. "But I was forgetting, Mr. Inkston; the intricacies of our local politics must be very uninteresting matter for you, and I have to request that you hot-brained children will not renew the subject in my presence."

O'Hara saw at once that his father was impervious to further argument, and another cloud flitted across his horizon.

But he had little time for reflection that evening—there were so many things to be said on all sides, so many minutiæ of home and college life to be talked over, and so many plans perfected to make the vacation a pleasant one.

And when at length the party did retire, after discussing to the full those cheery prospects, Charlie O'Hara had almost forgotten his grave speculations, and bent all his thoughts to the pleasures of the present.

CHAPTER V.

THE RIVAL CANDIDATES.

THE next morning broke crisp and frosty. The breakfast-room looked positively bright for once, despite its heavy oak pannellings, and the ponderous mould in which all the ancient furniture was cast. A laughing fire threw out its yellow glare in cheery golden streams, and the hospitable breakfast-table yielded the choicest and most savory odors.

And then there was something so heart-stirring in the wide prospect from the broad bay window—the snow all cleared away, and the feeble wintry sun gleaming joyously through the frosty air, and the entire mosaic of green upland, woody hill, and purple mountain, clothed in glittering, healthy hues.

Miss O'Hara had reason to be proud as she stood at the window, and with glowing cheek pointed out to Frank Inkston the winter beauties of Glengarra.

And prouder grew her look and brighter her eye as the familiar bay of the foxhounds broke the outward stillness, and the red-faced old huntsman, Andy, trotted up his howling pack on the wide plateau below.

"A glorious day for the hounds," cried the impulsive girl, hastily throwing up the window and calling out to the huntsman, "Hallo, there, Andy, where are we off to to-day?"

"Arrah! thin, is it yerself is there, Miss Milly?" shouted the huntsman, with an admiring glance at his fair interlocutor. "A sunny day to you, my darlin' child. We'll thry Knockmeelish to-day, an' the divel is in the dice if we don't get out a couple o' red fellows."

"Oh! delightful!" cried Miss O'Hara. "The finest gallop in the country, Mr. Inkston, and a certainty of a day's sport." And she glided away like a sunbeam to array herself in hunting costume.

Inkston hastened away to follow her example, and in less than an hour such a gala crowd as brightened the park could only be equalled in those days of Ireland's sporting pre-eminence.

Nearly the only things about Glengarra that escaped the effects of the owner's indolence were the foxhounds and the stud. The Glengarra park was ever esteemed the noblest in the county, and the Glengarra stables yielded to none in the breed and "going" powers of their occupants. They were, in fact, one of Mr. O'Hara's chief connections with the neighboring gentry; for, even though they seldom entered his house, and seldomer still partook of his hospitality, they cheerfully followed his hounds, which had the reputation of hunting the most sporting ground, and starting the best game to be had in Tipperary.

So on this morning especially "the meet" was most numerous. The irregular crowd of red-coats, spread away over the grassy lawn, included the *crême de la crême* of the neighboring aristocracy, and the fair occupants of the carriages were among the lights and leaders of county society.

We are concerned with but few of the gay throng. Emily O'Hara, in her simple black costume and enchanting joyousness, everyone knew. Our hero, too, was having a pleasant time, shaking hands by the hundred, exchanging kindly salutes with the ladies, and introducing on all sides his handsome friend from Dublin, who comported himself with all the polished courtesy that distinguished him in society.

Our gigantic friend, Captain Jack Colthurst, was likewise there, mounted on a big-boned animal like himself, and showering jovial banter on all sides of him. But Jack had a disagreeable game to play to-day, and but for his towering figure and imposing riding-whip would have probably been worsted. For the rumor, that he would contest the county in the popular interest, arrayed against him the whole powerful battalion of aristocratic society. The pompous dowagers in the carriages administered him the most refined and subtle insults; the gentlemen paid him the blunter compliment of turning aside when he approached.

But Jack Colthurst was not the man to be out of sorts under such treatment. Though now only the owner of a little estate swamped by debts and mortgages, he was representative of one of the proudest ancestral houses that man could boast of. His French education had further given him a distaste for aristocratic distinctions; and, without ever giving himself the trouble of hating anybody, he was always able to overpower sour temper and disarm insult. So his boundless fund of humor overflowed the petty annoyances of the Tipperary magnates, and he flitted about through the red-coated crowd with as much ease and laughing pleasure as if he were merely galloping over his own lawn field.

Mr. O'Hara was on the ground—just to put in a appearance; but he was too careworn and too sick to take part in the sport. He never hunted now, and the deep-mouthed bay of the foxhound rather offended his sensitive temper, so he speedily made his excuses, and disappeared from a scene of enjoyment in which he could not share.

The only other member of the hunt with whom we

have to do was Lord Crabshawe, the aristocratic nominee for the representation of the county. In later times Mr. Sothern has given us, in his "Lord Dundreary," an exact reproduction of his lordship. He was a dandy every inch—brainless, stupid, vicious—a senseless puppet, propped up on a pedestal of wealth and title—a hater of everything Irish, unless Irish girls—a perfect type of the Anglo-Irish Plutarch. But he lived, slept, and acted in a besetting languor. This dreamy stupidity might almost be taken for amiability; but the quickness with which he awoke at the call of sensuous passion removed the illusion, and left him to stand on his own bare claims to friendship—broad acres and a proud family title.

Now Lord Crabshawe had been educated at Eton, had seen what was to be seen on the continent, and had grown a moustache—a languid, sickly streak of hair just darkening the pinkish-white complexion on which he prided himself so immensely. Of course, he was not himself a stranger to such varied attractions. He didn't ambition the name of genius, nor did he stoop to making himself brilliant. He considered his birth, wealth and beauty ought to be supreme proof to the world that he was a very desirable man to make acquaintance with. And he was not far mistaken, for the world is largely composed of people who care very little for those vulgar things called virtues, provided that men's failings are labelled with a coat-of-arms and a money-box.

A short period before the commencement of our tale, his lordly father had been compelled to shake off this mortal coil, and Lord Crabshawe settled down into the ancestral moorings, to all appearance one of the most comfortable men in the county. To be sure, the first step towards the maintenance of the paternal dignity was that he should become M. P. for Tipperary. The post had been an heir-loom in the family for generations, and, with the present lord's mighty territorial influence, seemed certain to remain so.

Not that Lord Crabshawe either knew or cared anything for politics. He never occupied himself with subjects so *ennuyants*. Perhaps he would not raise his eyebrows if some one told him New Zealand was an island in Connemara. The war *in France* might certainly be taking place in Bantry Bay for aught he knew. But it was essential to his dignity that M. P. should be in his train of titles, and he had besides a reverential animosity to popular representation.

So he was highly shocked when he realized the rumor that Captain Colthurst, a mere Franco-Irish adventurer, was going to raise the standard of mob-law under the very nose of his nobility, and he swore—no, he didn't swear anything in particular, he only swore a Catholistic anathema, and quaffed his Madeira with his wonted listlessness. For Lord Crabshawe, of Crabbenden, son of a peer, deputy-lieutenant, landlord, and the rest of it, never dreamed that fortune meant any serious affront to his happiness by conjuring up this upstart democrat. In this unruffled forecast he was confirmed by his aristocratic friends, and more especially by Mr. O'Hara, who, as an old friend of his father, rather liked the young lord for his unexacting habits of reserve. The young lord in return rather liked Mr. O'Hara, but he assuredly liked his daughter, and felt piqued that his little attentions to Milly evoked no satisfactory response.

But love matters, like everything else, Lord Crabshawe took very much at his ease. He did not admire marriage as an institution—thought it imposed a good deal too much trouble—but he never doubted his ability, at any moment, to command the hand even of Milly O'Hara.

Nor was he very much discomfited, this bracing hunting morn, to find that even his base democratic rival received a greater share than he of the smiles of the wild beauty. He didn't see any great slight to his vanity in that—for weren't all the aristocratic belles around him paying him the most devoted attentions, and might he not have plucked any of these fair roses at any moment?

Still he kept dangling about the circle of admirers formed around Miss O'Hara, and he ventured an occasional observation with more than ordinary *empressement*.

Their talk was of the weather, the prospects of the day, the covers; but it at last floated out of these safe drydocks, and splash! down it came into the very vortex of election bitterness. It couldn't be otherwise, for Jack Colthurst was there, and so delightfully at his ease that everybody felt it a duty to disturb him.

"The election!" suggested some anonymous being.

"Aw, that's very true," lisped his lordship, with an easy effort to seem unconcerned. "They tell me, Captain Colthurst, you have some ideaw of—a—of, in fact, opposing me for the county."

"Idea! my lord," laughed Colthurst, "I've engaged ten big drums and two editors already. If that's not more than an idea I must have been an infernally lazy scoundrel."

"Yawz, very true," said his lordship, with infantile innocence, "yawz, the big drums especiallly. By Jove! ha! ha! Then, I suppose, you're quite serious?"

"Well, serious as a man that's going to eat his dinner, at any rate."

"Oh! gracious!" ejaculated Miss Whimper, in a tone of deep concern, not, of course, meant for his lordship. "The idea of siding with this horrible rabble, and against Lord Crabshawe, especially!"

"Horrible!" said her sympathizing mother.

"Disgraceful!" muttered a man's voice behind Colthurst.

"I beg your pardon!" and with the quickness of lightning he turned in the direction whence the voice proceeded,—but his great flashing eyes were enough — no one took up the challenge. "Ah! I thought some one was making an impertinent observation, and impertinent observations I don't relish, even when among *friends*"— this, with broad and undisguised humor. "We are likely to be on anything but good terms during this election; but I beg of you all to keep your tempers. You know it is just possible a man may differ with you all, and yet not put you to the guillotine on your own front-gates à *la mode Française*."

"Oh! gracious!" cried an old dowager who had not quite followed the speaker, but picked up a whole world of horrors in the allusion to the guillotine.

"I confess I can't see your distinction, Mr. Colthurst," said a sour-faced little J. P., who habitually ignored Jack's French military grade. "Those who stir up a horde of rebels and assassins against their natural masters might go farther."

"Yes, they might teach those rebels and assassins how to get enough to eat," cried Miss O'Hara, impulsively.

"What!" exclaimed Lord Crabshawe, with languid alarm, "is Miss O Hara, too, going ovaw to the enemy?"

"Shocking!" chimed in Miss Whimper, sympathetically.

"Oh! don't be alarmed, your lordship," said Milly, with a merry laugh, "believe me, I should never hear of *your* being guillotined without praying for your *post mortem* felicity."

"How kind!" exclaimed his lordship, stroking his feeble moustache in a misty effort to analyze the compliment.

"Yawz, thank you; I hope Captain Colthurst will be as merciful;" and he sneered with delicious self-satisfaction.

"Oh! as for that," said the individual addressed, "I can tender you my best wishes for your success—in the other world, as a grandfather of mine said to a man he was going to fight a duel with. But even in this I fear I will be running with heavy weights. Let's hope we may not break one another's heads before we reach the winning-post."

The conversation was interrupted by the loud blast of the huntsman's horn, as he marshalled his pack along the road to the Knockmeelish cover.

The party broke up into little knots on the way, and while the rival candidates kept dangling round the sweet heiress of Glengarra, talking stupid politics, Charles O'Hara had piloted Inkston into a little circle of chatty girls and fox-hunting dunderheads, among whom the brilliant young student soon raised himself to the dignity of a small Solomon.

At length the gay cavalcade reached Knockmeelish, and spread themselves along the base of the sloping hill whose side was clothed with the bushy underwood of the cover. The dogs pierced through the furze brakes, and pantingly scoured the hill.

Then there was a thrilling yowl from the far end of the cover, and a wild shout of "Tally-ho" as the dogs dashed off in pursuit. Almost instantaneously the cry of "There, he's out!" and the baying of hounds, came from the opposite side of the copse, and it was immediately discovered that two foxes had been simultaneously unearthed. Uncertain in what direction the hunt really lay, the whole field started off on the track of the dogs they found nearest, and while some went one way, others took the opposite direction, so that the hunt was speedily broken up into two main parties, who, in the excitement of the chase, held their course onward whither the inspiriting bay of the fox-hounds invited them.

O Hara and Frank Inkston tailed off with one party, while Miss O'Hara, Lord Crabshawe, and Captain Colthurst joined the other.

Among the few good qualities grudgingly allowed to the Irish gentry of the last century, they have gained an undisputed reputation for pre-eminence in the chase; and we are ourselves orthodox believers in the breakneck propensities of "The Galway Blazers." Whether 't is the impulsiveness of the Celt, or the tempting stone walls, or the conviction that suicide is the only solace left to ostracized Ireland, we don't care to decide; but the fact stands, that the children of the Green Isle have acquired a reputation all over the world for risking their skins wherever such an amusement is to be had— on a battle-field, or over a double-ditch. Yet, sooth to say, the twenty or thirty red-coated gentry that followed in the train of what we call Miss O'Hara's party, were, for the most part, very indifferent equestrians— that is, if we are to conclude (as, of course, we ought not) that their postern grip of the saddle was a measure of precaution, and that their quiet detours to the gaps were inspired by a plebeian reverence for ox-fences. But it must also be borne in mind that most of them were on the shady side of forty; and, if they did not, all of them, fly pell-mell over hedges and ditches, most of them, at all events, managed to keep their toggery untainted.

So much for the rule; exceptions, however, there

were, and our readers will scarce need the assurance that Jack Colthurst was one who quickly made his way to the van. Miss O'Hara, too, was none of your pasteboard horsewomen. Mounted on a magnificent charger, a few strides sufficed to give her first place, and with glowing eye and mantling cheek she dashed in on the track of the hounds, ahead of the entire field. And who next? Was it a vague foreshadowing of events, or merely one of those thousand queer coincidences we come across every day, that Lord Crabshawe and Captain Colthurst should run abreast in pursuit of the fair leader?

It was so, at all events; and, from the very first bay of the hounds, the chase shaped itself most perceptibly into a strange allegory of the contest between the rivals. Ride where Lord Crabshawe might, he found himself locked in a contest with the popular candidate; and did it awake any reflection, the fact that both seemed striving after the beauteous prize whose lithe figure fled away slightly in advance? The idea struck Colthurst as an odd one, and without time to pause over it, he somehow yielded himself to it for the moment.

And with the cool air fanning his purpose, and the buoyant life surging up to his temples, he gave loose reins to his imagination and his steed, and bounded away over the crisp turf as in a mad struggle for life and death.

Even his phlegmatic lordship caught the infection—for the bracing air of a hunting morning dissipates the most frigid cynicism—and without acknowledging to himself that he was in earnest, he found himself flying, with more and more rapidity, without the power to rein in his alarms.

Had it been a mere struggle of physical strength between the young men, the result could not be for one moment in peril; but the superiority of Lord Crabshawe's horse out-balanced the noblest efforts of Jack Colthurst's horsemanship, and to his chagrin the latter found himself powerless to outstrip the spanking pace of his lordship's thorough-bred; while the beautiful girl in front improved her pace to a maddening flight, and kissed a smiling farewell to the struggling rivals.

On they flew over the broad fields, up hill and down, through the rushing air, to the deep music of the foxhounds, and still they held the same places in this curious struggle.

The chase had reached the boiling point of excitement, and with every nerve strained, every eye flashing, and every heart throbbing, the whole field were sweeping on in headlong career, when a sharp turn at the base of a woody hill brought Miss O'Hara in full view of an obstacle that might well have paralyzed a stouter heart.

Some twenty yards on, the woody hill they were skirting broke into a steep and narrow gorge, with sharp-cloven sides, studded with gnarled stumps and jutting rocks. At the nearest entrance of the defile, a rude fence of heavy oak saplings rose to the height of five or six feet. At the far side of this formidable barrier, a brawling stream, rushing in a white cataract from the hill, tumbled away over its rocky bed, and after passing the noisy lagoon formed in the hollow, made its way down to the meadows by the edge of the opposite hill. Beyond the stream the ground was rugged in the extreme, and piled with unshapely boulders.

It was through this treacherous gorge that Reynard and his hot pursuers fled, and it was towards it Miss O'Hara found herself now irresistibly hurried. She was a brave girl—so brave that scarce an atom of

feminine weakness showed itself in her nature—but to
be thus brought at an instant's notice within view of an
obstacle which she too well knew to be insuperable,
was too much even for her fortitude. And an icy chill
shot across her heart in that brief flash of reflection.

But to draw back was impossible. She was already
within a few springs of the leap—her brave steed
swelling every muscle in the mad excitement—her own
soul thrilled with all the passion of the chase, and a
whole field of famed riders waiting to " be shown the
way " by *her!*

During this brief interval of contemplation, Captain
Colthurst and Lord Crabshawe had turned the corner
almost together. They saw the brave girl flying on to
that fearful leap, and the whole danger flashed across
both of them at once!

But the idea of danger only soberized his lordship's
temporary enthusiasm, and suggested immediate measures of discretion for himself, while Colthurst feared
that any outcry on his part would only aggravate the
danger by unnerving the object of his solicitude.

Another moment and precaution was too late! With
a joyous cry that thrilled Colthurst to the very soul, the
gallant girl rose her horse to that appalling leap. They
rose together like a flash over the great barrier of
timber! yes, over, but not beyond! Her one moment
of tremulousness had stayed the powers of the horse,
and splash! went rider and steed into the noisy stream
below.

The agony of that moment would, in calmer moments have assured Jack Colthurst of his wild love
for Miss O'Hara. But there was small time for reflection. He was already almost abreast of the fence himself, and alive to the dread peril that lay before him.
Concern for himself was his last thought, but the fear

that he might be too late to save *her*—that he might even injure her in the jump—ah! these were the thoughts that put spurs to his resolution.

With the eagle eye of a military man, he chose his ground a little above where Miss O'Hara had taken the jump. With a wild hurrah! and a gigantic lift, he faced his good steed to the trial. A moment of rushing thoughts, and he found himself safe on the opposite bank. His horse, indeed, had stumbled, and he was himself conscious of some painful twitchings in the ribs; but in this supreme moment of joy, he thought not of himself. Staggering to his feet, he plunged into the stream. There was the light drapery still floating away, and still clinging unconsciously to the powerless horse.

One struggle, and he had the yielding form of the fair girl in his arms, and was striving with mad energy for the bank.

A quick glance showed him that she had sustained no dangerous injuries. His brandy-flask soon sent the red life coursing through the white cheeks; and before he had time to look around for assistance, Miss O'Hara had opened her great eyes in immediate perception of what had happened.

"Ah! Jack," she said, with a faint smile, clinging to the huge form that clasped her. "I'm glad 'twas you! 'Twill be nothing. A little more of that brandy, Jack. There now, millions of thanks, I'm quite myself again!" and without any more dramatic awakenings, she leaped lightly, though somewhat painfully to her feet, regaining in a moment her whole flood of life and joyousness.

"Oh! but wasn't it stupid?" she asked, half-laughingly, as she shook the water from her long, black tresses. "Papa will be making such a dreadful fuss about it, though I don't believe I'm one iota the worse of the little adventure.

"You did it gallantly, Milly," cried Colthurst, enraptured by the happy turn of events, "I could have died for the girl that would have taken that jump as you did."

"Oh! but it's much better for you to live for her, Jack," laughed the happy girl, with a light rosy flush, nevertheless, overspreading her face. "Indeed, 'twasn't my fault or your own that they are not 'waking' you at present. But, in all seriousness, are you in any way hurt?"

"Pshaw! what would hurt *me*, my dear child? but *you* must surely be injured?"

"Not at all. Now that I examine myself, I don't find even a scratch to talk of. Ah! but poor Hercules! Poor brute, he bore all the brunt of the fall. What *has* happened him?"

"Ah! poor wretch! he has fared worse than any of us. He's had his neck broken."

"What a pity! But, see, bless my soul, if this isn't Lord Crabshawe riding up! He surely hasn't taken that jump?"

It *was* Lord Crabshawe, riding up in unruffled dignity; but he had *not* taken that jump. He was coming from the other side, whither he had reached by an easy passage farther down the hill. He approached the pair with all the appearance of a man of superior wisdom.

"O Miss O'Hara!" he drawled out, with easily affected concern, as he approached, "I'm so delighted—you're not hurt—are you?"

"Oh! no," said Miss O'Hara, with the suspicion of a sneer, "your kind care has preserved me."

"Yawz, indeed, I was awfully shocked. 'Twas mad, mad! Yawz, perfectly mad! I tried a thing of that soawt befoaw, and I found it—you know—I found it didn't do."

"So you didn't do it this time, your lordship," said Colthurst, with a burst of laughter.

Jack's merry laugh touched his lordship's dignity extremely. He never liked anyone to laugh at *him*, and it was especially annoying coming from one who, he mistily realized, had already vanquished him in one quarter.

"Captain Colthurst might find reason to believe that I *could* do it, at all events," he at last said with pompous coolness; then, finding that even this burst only provoked a new peal of good-humored laughter from the captain, his dignity at length forsook him, and, turning on his heel, he muttered, "Demned insulting! just what might be expected!"

"Oh! if that's your idea, my lord," cried Jack, with unfeigned contempt, "I wish you joy with the insult, and make you a present of a whole dozen of 'em. But we are cruel brutes to be keeping you here, Miss O'Hara," turning to the young lady, "you must be quite drenched, and you'll want an immediate change, if you don't want a six-weeks' fever. Come, dear, and we'll strike out for the nearest cabin. As for Lord Crabshawe, he needn't have brought us his ill-humor as he didn't bring us his help. He ought to know that I am always at home and ready to have a quiet *tête-a-tête* with people who don't know how to be civil."

His lordship was boiling. He felt himself foiled, buffeted, at his rival's feet; yet he was powerless to do or say anything. Insults, like dinners, and in fact like everything else with Lord Crabshawe, required digestion, and pending that, he unburdened himself in one long and pregnant malediction on mankind generally; then swore something terrible between his teeth, and then—decamped with all due haste and stupidity.

The rest of the hunt had come up in time for the double mortification of seeing their pet lord unmercifully snubbed, and the democratic champion unquestionably glorified. They were, of course, all delighted at Miss O'Hara's singular escape, and charmed with Captain Colthurst's bravery. But in other words, they very plainly intimated that they considered Miss O'Hara's jump as the act of a madcap, and Miss O'Hara's self a person far too flighty for domestic joys; while, as to Captain Colthurst, they hinted sundry cruel things about—well, only about his rebellious "continuations," which had broken loose during his watery campaign. Miss Fitztarem, fat, unfair, and thirty, who rode a palfrey and talked piety, was eloquent on the unwomanliness of such a dare-devil escapade. Miss Whimper, who was poetic, suggested, with an infallible cure for involuntary shower-baths, that, indeed, it was anything but unpleasant to set handsome young gentlemen breaking their necks after one. Old Tiger, a new-fledged landlord, erstwhile attorney and stockjobber, couldn't imagine what her papa would say. An expectant young subaltern, a suitor himself for Miss O'Hara's hand, spoke pathetically of the misfortune that had snapped his stirrup-rein, and hindered him from being "first at the death," as he blunderingly called it.

But Jack Colthurst's greatest mortification was the freezing civility with which Mr. O'Hara received from him the news of his daughter's rescue. The fact was, the whole occurrence had been grossly discolored by Lord Crabshawe, who had thoroughly poisoned the old man's mind, by misty hints and inuendoes, against his triumphant rival. And, though Mr. O'Hara strained his fair daughter to his breast in the fulness of paternal affection, and betrayed a depth of emotion that now rarely escaped his iron frame, he manifested rather pain than pleasure at the enthusiastic flow of gratitude with which the fair girl loaded Jack Colthurst in her father's presence.

He thanked Coltburst, of course—he was too polished not to be even refined in his compliments—but every word of gratitude was, as it were, sicklied over with a chilly hauteur that made his compliments fall like so many ice-bolts on the heart of their recipient.

The great warm heart of the young soldier shrunk from this last crowning exhibition of aristocratic ingratitude. He did not rate his own services very highly—but that his services, such as they were, should only serve to heighten the ingratitude of the man who owed him his daughter's life—this was a phenomenon that he failed to reason out.

And, for once, his flood of buoyant life was checked. In coldest language he declined the invitation to dinner, coldly extended by the lord of Glengarra, and, with a haughty farewell to father and daughter, he turned his horse's head from their house, sensible that he had met with one of the first real disappointments of his life.

CHAPTER VI.

MUTTERINGS OF FATE.

CAPTAIN Colthurst *was* out of temper—there was no mistake about it—as he drove through the long avenue at Glengarra Park. He had lived in the midst of busy scenes all his lifetime, and was never much addicted to contemplation; but the utmost resources of his gay temperament failed to drive away the sad thoughts that came thumping at his heart—thoughts of broken hopes, of disturbing loves, of innumerable unpleasant things, commingled in dim shades of evil—and, failing either to whistle away, or to think down, or even account for such strange forebodings, he adopted his usual alternative and became savage.

Yes, the luxury of savagery stole over his heated brain until he lost all consciousness of civilization. He spurred and slashed his unfortunate horse until he broke into a maniacal gallop; he tore through the thick canopy of trees as if the boughs were not smiting and tearing him at every step; and he would doubtless have broken his bones over the great front gate but that he was stayed in his insane career by a loud burst of laughter, and a voice that he could not mistake.

With a savage feeling of joy that he had some one to fight with, he put the horse on its haunches with a sudden jerk, and found to his chagrin that he was face to face with Charles O'Hara, who, with Frank Inkston and another of the hunting party, was returning after the day's sport, entirely innocent of what had befallen the others.

Colthurst looked at them with a stare of disappointment, expressive of the thought that rose to his mind—"Confound ye, I thought 'twas some one I could have a row with"—which melancholy reflection was aggravated by the apparently resistless laughter with which he was saluted.

"I'm quite at your service, gentlemen," he said, at last, with a ludicrous attempt to seem dignified; "but as I'm not aware that I've turned into a monkey, ye'll excuse me for asking what the devil are ye laughing at?"

"Why, in heaven's name, what has happened you, Jack?" cried O'Hara, in the interval of a suffocating fit of laughter.

"Eh! happened?" exclaimed Colthurst, with a stupid stare.

He glanced at O'Hara for explanation—followed his eye to his own person—and then, rapidly recognizing the cause of their merriment, burst himself into a sympathetic roar of laughter, as he realized that one of his boots and part of his breeches were almost completely torn away, his linen floating through numerous crevices in his hunting coat, his whole attire still drenched with water and splashed with mud, and his hat bruised into the semblance of a mashed turnip.

The droll side of the disaster immediately re-aroused all Colthurst's humor, and he laughed with a heartiness that would be accountable were anyone else the victim.

"But, in God's name, what has happened you?" again asked O'Hara, convulsed with laughter.

"Oh! as to that," said Colthurst, "'t was simply a big toss over a double-ditch—one of those accidents of war that occasionally leave a fellow without a clean breeches. But that reminds me," he added, with a significant glance at O'Hara, "I shall want you to come home with me to bear witness that I didn't get my scars in bad company."

"Certainly, old fellow," said Charlie, immediately perceiving there was something in the wind. "Frank, you will excuse me for a few minutes. Mr. Campion and yourself can get on to the house. I'll be back in time for dinner."

The gentlemen bowed, and proceeded up the avenue, while Colthurst and O'Hara pursued their way at a walk close together. In a short, unembellished narrative, the captain explained to O'Hara the cause of his present plight, and then dwelt with more sadness on the additional estrangement his rescue of Milly had created between himself and her father.

O'Hara received the intelligence of his sister's escape with all the enthusiasm of his impulsive soul. He pressed Colthurst's hand until he seemed desirous of wrenching it off in gratitude; his manly face glowed with unspeakable thanks to the giant beside him; but every feeling gave way to one of anger and indignation, as he listened to the tale of his father's gratuitous exhibition of ingratitude.

"He is my father, Jack," he said, sadly, "and has always been a fond and indulgent father to me; but what you tell me would be almost sufficient to root out every filial affection from my heart."

"Oh! take it easy, my boy," returned the other, deeply touched at the ardent enthusiasm of his friend, "I'd never have told you a word about this if I thought you'd make such a rout about it. I suppose I needn't tell you I'd be the last in the world to encourage any-one to quarrel with his father, and especially you, who are blessed with so happy a home. No, my boy, that was not the object of my speaking to you. I have numerous matters which you and I must talk over very seriously, and as I don't see that this is a very proper opportunity, say to-morrow evening."

"Come, then, to tea, to-morrow evening, and you'll have Milly herself to thank you."

"Oh! no," said Colthurst, seriously, "I can never enter Glengarra again. I'm not a man to take affront at every haystack, but I have feelings of my own, and I don't care to have them trampled on."

"True, Colthurst," cried Charlie, with a warm grip of his hand, "and I'm not the man to ask you to be a second time insulted."

"At the same time, Charlie, you mustn't imagine that I'm a bit angry with your father. If 'twas only for your sake, and—and—Miss O'Hara's, I'll never have an unkind thought of him. But stay—oh! yes—you've promised to come over to see Lucy—say to-morrow evening, then, and I will be looking out for you most anxiously."

"With pleasure, my dear fellow," cried O'Hara, "I'll be with you, as sure as the clock. Meanwhile, my best respects to Miss Colthurst, and a host of adieux to you, my dear friend."

The friends parted with a hearty farewell, and O'Hara turned his horse's head homewards, with feelings sad and heavy beyond expression.

The short winter day had long since closed, and it was quite dark as he rode into the yard to get rid of his horse. At the gate he was accosted by Mick Hoolohan, whose face, despite manifest traces of inebriation, wore a far more serious aspect than usual. He beckoned his young master into one of the stables, and having assured himself that there was no one within earshot, whispered mysteriously into his ear.

"Do you know James?"

"Inkston's servant? Of course I do."

"Well, I don't."

"Confound you, you rascal!" cried O'Hara, annoyed at Mick's utter *nonchalance,* "you're drunk."

"Not a bit of it," returned Mick, with judicial serenity. "I don't mane to deny that I had a little dhrop; but I'm downright serious that I don't know James. An' what I was goin' to tell you is, that I'm afeerd you don't know him ayther."

"What are you driving at?"

"Just this, then, that I b'leeve him to be the knowin'est scoundrel that iver swung from a gallows."

"But what under the sun have I to say to that? I'm not his father confessor. If you think he'll steal the spoons or forks, why not tell some one whose business it is?"

"Listen to me for a few minnits; I know the fellow now for a good long spell, an' I niver could make anything out of him. I always had a kind of idaya that he couldn't have come o' dacent parints, or he needn't have the hang-gallows look he has; but the divil himself couldn't squeeze a word out of him more than 'yis, sir,' or 'no, sir,' like a parrit. Well, whin he come to Tipperary, I swore a holy oath I'd make him more jaynial; an be this book I *done* it."

"What did you do?"

"Why, I soused the bla'guard with potheen till he couldn't see a hole through a laddher, an' thin to hear him chatterin'! Be the hole in me coat, the fellow was like a big forge bellows, an' he laughed and grinned, an' swore, until I thought he'd dance a Highlan' jig on the table for pure divarshion. But the worst of it was, divil a syllable could I undherstand from him."

"What! he spoke in a foreign language?" asked O'Hara, his interest suddenly kindled.

"Sich gibberish I niver heard out of a rookery," said

Mick. "But though I know nothin' of furrin tongues, I'm sartin he was sayin' nothing good; for the light o' hell was playin' in the fellow's eyes, an' he used to throw up his hands like a play-acthor cryin' for vingeance, an' altogether he was such a divilish-lookin' object, that I was goin' to sprinkle holy wather on him, fearin' ivery minnit he'd go off in a flash o' fire. Take my word for it, Misther Charles, that same James is the biggest bla'guard unhung; an' shure, if I might make so bould, the divil a much difference that way between masther an' man."

"What do you mean, fellow?" cried O'Hara, feeling at the same time a new feeling of indefinable dread creeping over him.

"Begor, sir, as you ask my opinion, I'll give it to you, wid a heart-an'-a-half. I had always my suspicions that there was somethin' dark about Mr. Inkston, an' that fellow James mutthered something very like your father's name in one of his big furrin curses."

"He did?"

"That he did, sir. I hope you won't be offinded wid me, Masther Charles, for makin' so bould; but, as an ould frind o' the family, begor, 'twas somethin' like the croon of a banshee, that fellow's murdherin' big words. I'd have broke his head on speculation, only I didn't like to, in regard to his masther's bein' a frind of yours."

"Well, Mick," said O'Hara with a smile, "I'm thankful to you for your anxiety on my account; but don't, like a good fellow, trouble yourself any more about the matter. Give James less whiskey punch, and ye'll probably get on better together;" and having handed over his horse to one of the stable boys, he ended the interview.

Nevertheless, despite his gayety, Mick's odd observations had not been without their effect on him, more especially as they came in concert with the gloomy thoughts with which Colthurst's narrative had filled his mind. And throughout the evening this impalpable gloom dispelled all his natural gayety.

The dinner, indeed, passed off in an atmosphere of entire unrest. The light and soul of the party was removed.

Miss O'Hara excused herself by saying she felt unwell after her day's excitement, and locked herself up in her own little boudoir. And she *must* have been unwell to no ordinary degree, though she complained of no injuries, for her face had lost all its rosy flush, and her eyes—yes, even those laughing, sparkling eyes—were red with weeping; and with her white hand pressed wearily against her forehead, she sat moveless at the open window, gazing down listlessly into the dark night, until the pale stars came out flickering in the frosty sky, and the round moon gilded her black locks with a silver aureole. There was something at Miss O'Hara's heart besides the casuality of the day.

Mr. O'Hara preserved his usual composure, and his polite show of gayety; but it was easy to note, by the deeper-furrowed cheeks and clouded brow, that his thoughts were not of the pleasantest.

Even Frank Inkston's face told more than it ordinarily did, and Charlie felt a sort of sympathetic pleasure in the omnipresent dulness.

The dinner was hurried over by mutual consent; and the wine went round and round without working a change in the uncheering monotony. The adventure of the day was studiously avoided, and every other topic of conversation seemed to be beset with similar difficulties. Even the blazing log-fire lost its cheering influence, and became part and parcel of the pervading drowsiness, conjuring up weird shadows on the panelled walls and in the recesses of the dusky curtains.

O'Hara felt, as he had never felt before, nervous, uneasy, and sad. Little wonder that he worked up the spirit of the scene into some vague shadow of fate.

Silence at last settled over the little group, and everybody sat staring at nothing, and gliding into strange dreams, until it became unbearable, and retirement became indispensable.

Mr. O'Hara bid them his usual "good-night," and left the friends alone ere they also retired.

What wondrous power was it that seemed to link together the thoughts of these young men? Inkston was especially moved. His commonplace smile was frozen up; there was something terrible, yet pleading in the glare of his eyes.

"Good-night, dear friend — good-by!" at length he said, in a tone of solemnity; and seizing O'Hara's hand he wrung it with a warm clutch that nearly set the blood spouting from his finger-ends.

"Good-night!" — and they parted — parted on the dark sea of trouble, without compass or sail to guide their toilsome course—parted on the wide ocean of probabilities, so soon to meet amid its stormy billows.

And the murmurings of fate sounded through that house with voice as distinct and tone as piercing as ever fabled banshee.

CHAPTER VII.

LORD CRABSHAWE ON THE DUELLO.

Lord Crabshawe sat in his great arm-chair in the library of Crabbenden Manor, indicating plainly in face, gesture, and posture that he was out of humor. Ill-temper was with his lordship a chronic complaint; it was the usual resource of his dull hours, and he sometimes affected it as an addition to his dignity. But those intermittent attacks were of a mitigated character, extending not into his own inmost feelings. They were rather a languid kind of amusement—it cost so little, and was so soothing to see everyone about him tearing mad, from the outraged tom-cat to the insulted footman.

But his present visitation of bad humor was far more virulent. A feeling of his own—and one of his most cherished, too—had been touched, and the mighty exquisite lay writhing in the first real woe thrown on the pathway of his gilded life. The adventure of the hunting-field gave a sudden rise to all his dormant passions. Before, he had been rather too lazy to be wicked than radically good; now, the great mass of his indolence and stupidity was broken through by this crushing blow to his dearest pretensions.

Lord Crabshawe could have disdained Captain Colthurst had he confined himself merely to political opposition, for the former never doubted his ability to annihilate the latter at the poll. But where his name and wealth ceased to have influence—where the contest narrowed itself to one of personal honor—there it was that all the ire of Lord Crabshawe's soul was awaked, for there he felt himself worse than helpless.

If he had searched his heart the day before to know if he was a coward, he would doubtless have acquitted himself in all conscientiousness—for the lily-liver was so coated with gold, and rank and arrogance, that even to himself it was a most valorous looking organ. But it was quite another thing now, when this meretricious corslet was torn away, and when man had to confront man on an equal and unsheltered platform.

Yes, decidedly he *was* a coward, shivering without his social armor as a turkey-cock might without his feathers. The worst of it was, he could no longer disguise it from himself, and quite innocently he found himself casting up a pile of death's heads and bleeding corpses until he found the prespiration blinding him.

And then, heedless of the chafe to his proud soul, he weighed the matter over again to see whether he could not retire on his well-fortified dignity. But it was no use; the same conclusion forced itself inevitably upon him—he must fight this detested Colthurst.

Nineteenth-century humanitarians will, perhaps, find some difficulty in following him to this dread ultimatum; but, according to the canons of society at that date, it is easily intelligible, for the duel was the invariable arbiter of "points of honor," and "points of honor" were so flexibly understood that they might mean anything at the whim of either of the duellists.

It is true that Lord Crabshawe, any more than Captain Colthurst, laid no special claim to the right of fighting on account of Miss O'Hara, beyond a general notion that as he had conceived a vague sort of fancy for her no one else should dare cross his desires. But he felt sure that Colthurst's daring leap was an open affront to himself, and his subsequent insults, in presence of a crowd who had been trained to look up to him as a half deity, decided his lordship that there was no choice between fighting and dishonor.

Now, there was a multiplicity of circumstances tending to bring out his innate cowardice into strong relief. One was his inveterate indolence, which taught him to look on the exertion of fighting a duel, with its many disagreeable chances, as an intolerable nuisance. Another was, that his opponent should have the double guilt of being a democrat and a first-rate shot—a murderous combination against which he dare not, even in imagination, oppose his own kid-glove manipulation of firearms. But a third was probably the most powerful, and it was, that he was extremely comfortable as he was, with his lion's share of this world's goods, while the prospect of being suddenly transferred to other spheres, where he was not sure that fire and brimstone might not supersede feather beds, was so distasteful that he contemplated an early course of studies in the Book of Common Prayer.

His imagination sharpened by the circumstances, he ran over the whole bead-roll of possible disasters in an incredibly short space of time, until he had gathered round him an overpowering nightmare of blazing pistols, amputated legs, blood-stained deperadoes, and a thousand other horrid creations of his disordered brain.

It is hardly necessary to say that those disturbing thoughts ruffled considerably his lordship's ordinary infantile placidity. He cursed and swore when argument failed to appease his terrors. He kicked about chairs and tables until there wasn't one available in healthy condition. Then he cursed the servants to his heart's content; and finding all those remedies powerless to drive away that ugly twitching about the throat, occasionally experienced by the *guileless*, he at length embraced his *dernier ressort*, and " drowned his sorrows in the flowing bowl."

The usual effect of his potations on Lord Crabshawe was to exhilarate him; and it was with this object he now " sainted the spigot " with so much devotion. But exhilaration would not come. On the contrary, every bowl of the fiery brandy that he gulped down only dulled his intellect, while his cowardly apprehensions grew more appalling.

Such was his state of mind when " Captain Crofts " was announced, and a middle-aged, square-built, moustached gentleman strode into the room and saluted his lordship with an alarmingly affectionate shake-hands.

Lord Crabshawe looked and felt as if his visitor was an undertaker. There was, indeed, a close resemblance between that necessary nuisance's smirk and the bland smile of the captain; and his lordship was already shuddering at the thought of the business-like way in which this benign military gentleman would consign him to six feet of earth.

Indeed, the thought was not a very extravagant one, for though Captain Crofts did not follow the undertaker's craft, his ordinary avocations were, to the weak-minded, almost equally funereal. He was, in fact, second-in-ordinary to every duel fought in the south riding of Tipperary, and the reader may be assured that this commission was no very limited one at a time when people fought duels almost as frequently as they shake hands in our own days.

But duelling was Captain Crofts' profession, and, beyond an irregular pension, his only visible means of livelihood. He had slaughtered a full half-dozen himself at twelve paces, and told numerous pleasant little anecdotes of his prowess at the ill-defined period when he was serving in the Low Countries against France—both attributes which, added to a defiant swagger and a blustering tone of voice, established his reputation as a villain of the first magnitude on an imperishable basis.

He was such a man of the world—so infallible a tribunal on points of honor—so well "up" in the regulations of the duello—and such a jolly companion over a fellow's last bottle, that to have him secured as "friend" was esteemed a victory in itself, even if the "friendship" should end in a perforated heart or an abbreviated leg.

To be sure, it was insinuated that his friendship was a thing of £ s. d. Malicious people even noted that he had never been "second" to a poor man, and——Well, never mind, we won't give currency to any more of the slanders on this friend of humanity.

Of course, Lord Crabshawe divined in a moment what he wanted. Like a vulture, he was always sure to be hovering round when there was death in the wind.

"My dear Lord Crabshawe," he began, wreathing his face with smiles, and helping himself in the most amiable manner to a generous measure of brandy, "it was only a minute ago I heard of your affair with Colthurst"——

"I knew it," muttered his lordship with a despairing shudder.

"Of course you did," continued the other, not exactly following Lord Crabshawe's train of thought, "I did not lose a moment when I heard it. Said I to myself, 'Crabshawe will bring down that fellow like a bird—twould be a pleasure to be *his* second.'"

"Aw! ha! ha!" responded Lord Crabshawe, with a most consumptive smile, roused into momentary valor by the spur to his vanity, and swallowing another tumbler-full of brandy to smother his apprehensions.

"Of course you *must* fight the fellow?" half asked Captain Crofts in a tone of the blandest complacency.

"Oh! of course you must fight the fellow," repeated Lord Crabshawe, mechanically, for he had relapsed deep into his cogitations on "graves, and worms, and epitaphs."

"Just as I expected," said Captain Crofts, feeling, nevertheless, and showing that another quantum of the fiery liquor was due him to compensate for his host's lukewarmness. "I knew you'd fight him. Of course 'tis a highly disagreeable duty, that of putting a bullet through a fellow, but "——

"Oh!" ejaculated his lordship with sincere fervor.

"But honor is honor, sir," said the captain, with the air of a man who had propounded some sublime doctrine, "and when upstarts of his sort—adventurers, sir—mere adventurers"—he thundered, in convenient ignorance of his own antecedents—"when they forget they have gentlemen to deal with—and when, as in your case, I presume, rascals knock decent people down "——

"Oh! no blows!" cried Lord Crabshawe, in the feeble hope that the distinction might avert the stern decree of honor.

"Well, 'twas quite as bad," observed the captain with a pleasant smile. "When such things will be allowed to go unpunished, the whole fabric of society will be levelled. I'm sure no one is more thoroughly alive to the importance of the occasion than yourself, my lord."

His lordship almost groaned at the aptitude of the remark.

"I'm sure you'll have no difficulty in winging him. In fact, the only difficulty now is the preliminary business, and that you know is always very delicate. I have grown tired of duels myself, and I've almost taken a vow that I never will shoot anybody else—for, somehow, hang it, five or six dozen people don't get killed without giving a fellow some trouble—but on this occasion I shall certainly make an exception in favor of your lordship. I'll be *your* second with the greatest pleasure."

"Yawz, second! But don't you think 'twould do as well to fire in the air?" This last remark was uttered in a total state of nervous aberration.

"In the air! Gracious goodness!"——

"O! not at all," cried his lordship, in trepidation at the mess he had made of it. "I only meant, wouldn't it—or—wouldn't it—oh! in fact, wouldn't you have another glass of brandy?"

The manœuvre would have been a good one only for his lordship's ashy face and tottering voice. As it was, Captain Crofts laughed at the joke, paid his attentions to the decanter, and, after a rapid survey of his host, came to the conclusion beyond all doubt, that he meant anything but fight.

Nor did this discovery seem to shock very much the valorous son of Mars; on the contrary, he grinned with all the more sincerity, and changed his tactics.

"There are a couple of things, however," he proceeded, "which are peculiar to this case, and it might be well to consider them before risking one's life needlessly."

Lord Crabshawe was on a sudden all ears—a faint star at last flickered in the gloomy future he had bodied forth from his own imaginings. Crofts smiled contentedly at his own foresight, and proceeded:

"First, then, we must bear in mind that this Colthurst is at best not what we call a gentleman, and could not therefore strictly claim the satisfaction of a gentleman."

"Ah!" ejaculated his lordship, who marvelled exceedingly that he had not thought of that before.

"But, then, I believe in your case that you're the insulted party, so I see no alternative but to thrash him."

"Oh!" groaned Lord Crabshawe, with a rueful elongation of face at the sudden collapse of his fine prospects.

"It would be much better if you could horsewhip him —*then* you needn't have the slightest compunction in refusing to fight; but I'm afraid Coltburst would be more than a match for most men at fisticuffs."

The tone of sympathy in which the captain couched these considerations inspired his lordship with a brilliant idea. Why could he not trust Crofts? He was evidently a man that could be discreetly silent at a fair premium.

"Crofts," he said, with plaintive sincerity, "can I trust you?"

Trust! For a friend like Lord Crabshawe he would pull down the moon or perish in the attempt!

"Wall, then, to confess honestly, ahem"—and his lordship blushed a deep vermillion, and twirled his moustache in perplexity. "In fact, you know—aw—"

"You needn't say another word, my lord," interrupted Crofts, evidently in high glee; "we understand one another perfectly. You don't like the idea of fighting Coltburst."

"Not—exactly—that——" stammered his lordship, still blushing at the confession.

"Oh! there's nothing extraordinary about it," said Crofts, in a tone of reassuring jocularity. "I've never met ten fellows in my life that, if their hearts were searched, didn't quail a little before a loaded pistol. I'm so old a hand at the trade myself now that I've come to look on firearms as a child would on his rocking-horse; but I may here confess to you in confidence, that at the first meeting I ever had—'twas with a French count or something, when our fellows were at Lieges—I acknowledge it without shame—I spent a whole day in devotions to some deity or other, in view of an immediate visit to the other world. Yes, sir, I think your hesitation on this occasion does very great credit to your refined sensibilities. Besides, we can't forget that Colthurst has had his training among a lot of rapscallions, who'd think little of firing before time—'tis a downright fact, sir—one of the fellows tried the trick on myself at one time, and I would'nt be here to tell it only that he killed my second instead of myself. So that I'm not a bit surprised that you're unwilling to fight him. Indeed, on consideration, I think it would be rather rash on your part."

"But his insults?" suggested Lord Crabshawe, who had been gathering his old nerve with every successive draught of consolation from the captain.

"Well," said the other, after a moment's contemplation, "I think that might be managed."

"Managed!" cried his lordship, cutting an impolite caper in the excess of his joy. "Crofts, you're a treazyaw! I always thought so. But how, my dear fellow, how?"

"Oh! in several ways," said Crofts, with the easy assurance of a Solon. "Of course, he must be punished, and that, if possible, without giving him an opportunity of punishing you."

"Always without dishonaw!" pronounced his lordship, with a grandiose, though somewhat ridiculous toss of the head.

"Oh! always without dishonor, to be sure—that is, to all the world. Well, let me see. Oh! I have it! The exact thing!"

"Well, well!" cried the impatient lord.

"Isn't Colthurst in debt?"

"Head-and-ears."

"Then challenge him—pay some of his creditors to have him put in custody before the time appointed—and then you can proclaim to the world with all confidence that he broke his engagement."

"Oh! exquisite! My dear captain, you're a genius—a regular genius. I shall never be able to thank you. It's capital! and, by George! can't we have him kept in till after the election, and send the fellow to the wall all at a crash?"

"Better again! Your right, on my honor. The fellow might give you some trouble during the election, and 'twill gall him like the very devil to be beaten at once on all points."

"Not that I'm afraid of the fellow," said Lord Crabshawe, to whom all his courage had at once returned, "and only that I don't caaw to be engaged in a squabble with low people, I really believe I should—ahem—I should horsewhip the rascal myself. But your plan is decidedly bettaw!"

"Oh! decidedly better," said Crofts, with an ambiguous sneer, "and much more feasible. But to be practical—do you know any creditor of his?"

"Fifty! There's Markham, the horse-dealer at Clonmel—he has a couple of decrees out against him"——

"That'll do admirably. I'll see Markham myself immediately. You won't be known in the matter at all. Ten pounds will settle it all. Now, let me see. This is Tuesday. The nomination for the county takes place on Friday. Nothing can be done to-night. We'll send Colthurst a challenge to-morrow to fight the morning after. Markham can send a couple of bailiffs to-morrow evening, and we'll have him lodged comfortably in Clonmel gaol when he should be fighting a duel and preparing for an election."

"Capital!" exclaimed Lord Crabshawe, in admiration.

"There's only one thing, though—that Colthurst isn't likely to give up without a tough fight; but never mind—I'll put them up to a dodge that will trap the bird nicely. Oh! won't it be a lesson to our democratic rascals to see their champion humbled to the dust!"

"Yawz!" said his lordship, now as defiant as ever. "I fancy 't will teach them that *I'm* not to be trifled with."

"Especially when you have a friend at your back," put in the other, with a sly leer.

"True, Crofts, how shall I ever repay you?"

"Oh! don't mention it, my lord," said Crofts. "I've done nothing that one friend might not expect from another. As the Duke of Cumberland said to me when our fellows were at Kloster Seven, 'Why, Crofts, I'd give you a regiment, only I'm afraid I'd insult you.' But, on my honor, that reminds me—those Grafton street people are annoying me infernally for some money they say I owe them—just a little trifle for carriages, I think, when I used attend court at the Castle. Would it be convenient to you to let me have £500 for a few days?"

Oh! certainly," cried his lordship, who was glad to be able to purchase his redemption at so little cost. "I'll draw you an order for £1,000 to-morrow."

"Thanks; 't will be a convenience until my March rents come in. But, here's the evening running away like a baker's horse. Fill your glass, my lord. What will we drink?"

"Here's to the devil!" shouted Crabshawe, on whom the liquor was beginning to tell.

"And all his angels," added Crofts, as he drained the glass—"'t would be too unselfish to forget ourselves."

CHAPTER VIII.

STORM-CLOUDS BREAKING.

WE doubt if it is entirely professional for a novelist to have sympathies beyond the due portraiture of his characters; and yet we could very gladly avoid the task of narrating the sad episodes now so near upon us, were it not that they have so vital a bearing on the development of the tale.

Charles O'Hara rose on the morning succeeding the hunt with an intolerable feeling of oppressiveness about his heart. He descended the broad staircase as in a feverish dream.

Mick Hoolohan was in waiting for him in the hall, and again the face of the faithful servant bore an appearance of anxious concern. Everything seemed to be putting on a robe of mourning.

"Oh! Masther Charles, I was just waitin' for you," he cried, when he espied his young master; "I told you yistherday to take care o' Misther Inkston, and be the mortial o' war, he's as mad as a March hare this minit!"

"What in the world do you mean?" demanded O'Hara, somewhat angrily.

"Come this way," replied Hoolohan, drawing the young man towards a postern door opening on the gardens; "he's walkin' up an' down the Arbor in the flower-garden since six o'clock this mornin' by himself, wavin' his hands in the air like a windmill, and swearin' out big furrin curses enough to pull down the house about him. An' if you were to see his face!—the Lord between us an' all harm—'tis as like the picture of the divel in Trinity as two pins—all blazin' like, an' still as white as a ghost. O! Masther Charles, there's somethin' wrong about him, believe me. Begor, I thought he was gettin' the hydherphobey, an' I was goin' to shoot him like a mad dog: but thin sometimes he'd stop his ravin' an' he'd look about quite nath'ral to see if there was anybody looking at him, and he'd bite his teeth like *thaw-shey*, an' thin he'd fold his arms till the fit kem on him agin. Come, for God's sake, an' see him yerself."

Led on by a resistless impulse, O'Hara rushed to the door, and was undoing the lock, when a servant came up.

"Misther O'Hara wants to see you immaydiately in the library, sir."

Like the sound of a funeral knell those few ordinary words chimed in with the gloomy thoughts now clustering in O'Hara's mind. He turned from the door without a word, and mounting a few flights of stairs, stood presently at the library door.

Crushing all his forebodings by a might of determination that he had scarcely believed himself possessed of, he hastily turned the handle and advanced into the room.

The old man was seated in an arm-chair opposite the fire, looking graver and sterner than ever.

"Take a chair," he commenced, with scant courtesy.

O'Hara felt that his anticipations were unwinding themselves into facts, but he did as he was desired, without betraying the slightest emotion.

His father scanned him searchingly, and proceeded:

"I have sent for you on an affair of very grave moment, to you—indeed, to both of us. I have always believed you to be enough of an O'Hara to have regard for honor and for truth. I ask you now to answer me two questions truthfully, as you regard my happiness and your own. I have heard that you are a member of the society of United Irishmen!"

"What!" interrupted O'Hara, astounded at the unlooked-for nature of the disclosure.

"I don't believe it myself," continued his father, the stern coldness of his glance growing more appalling as he noted the young man's flushed face—"I said I have only heard it. I have likewise heard that you intend to aid Captain Colthurst by every means in your power in the approaching election, contrary to my wishes."

"Father, who has told you this?" cried Charlie, now fully nerved for the whole shock.

"It is right that you should know," said his father, now rigid and cold-looking as marble. "This is my informant," and he placed in his son's hand a crumpled piece of paper, one side of which was covered with writing.

O'Hara glanced rapidly at the scroll. Then he started back as if smitten by lightning. The handwriting was rude, and the letters so uncouth as to appear written in a disguised hand. But not for one moment did they deceive O'Hara. He knew it too well—it was the handwriting of Frank Inkston!

Like a mountain torrent rushed a mad whirlwind of thought upon his brain, but in so bewildering a flood that they gave little chance for reflection. The one great question sprang uppermost—Why had Frank Inkston done this to *him*—him, who had cherished him as his dearest friend—who had never harbored the suspicions to which every one else yielded?

Nothing is more terrible than the reaction of the unsuspicious mind when it finds itself ensnared. In this brief moment of passionate agony, every particle of the mystery with which Inkston was surrounded occurred to him in torturing vividity; and, utterly unable to see his way through this dim maze, he yielded himself, with the relief of the fatalist, to the belief that it was the commencement of some dark plot of destiny's weaving.

He hastily perused the document in his hand. As we have said, it exhibited in orthography and calligraphy every evidence of a desire to screen the writer's identity. It read thus:—

"MR. O'HARA,—This ritin is from wan who takes a grate inthrest in yure fammily, and noin (knowing) yure been oposed to thrasun and rebbels, witch wud brin yure fammily into dizgrays, I now rite to tell you that yure sun, Masther Charless, is sworen a member of the united min, bein also goin to franse to bring over a frinsh army aginst the guvermint, as is well non (known) to the guvermint; an take my wurd for it, he'll be arrestid. Also, sur, he is goin to suport kaptin colethrust at the cownty eleckshin, bein goin to git all the tinnants on yure estate to go agenst yu for him. This is to waren yu thru frinship for yure fammily, but I don't like putin my name, so ask himself an he'll tell you this."

"Father, who has given you this?" cried the young man at length, casting the paper from him.

"Nobody," was the unmoved reply.

"Then how did you get it?"

"Ah! I see it interests you," said the father, and a deeper shade of displeasure crossed his knit brows. "But it concerns you deeply; it is right that you should know all about it. I found it here on my desk this morning. I neither saw nor know anyone in connection with it."

"Then you don't know that this handwriting is "——

What impulse was it that checked him as the name of

the writer rose to his lips? Whatever it was, he stopped abruptly.

"Is whose?" asked his father, shortly.

"It is no matter now; you do not know it."

"No," pursued the old man, the stern frown returning; "but what I want to know is whether the statements in that paper are true?"

"Yes, perfectly true," replied Charles, in a low tone.

"Heaven! Perfectly true!" repeated the old man, as if unconsciously; and as he spoke, Charles O'Hara noticed with alarm a deathly pallor closing over his face, and the iron frown relaxing into sickly furrows.

He sprang to his side, but the old man on the instant recovered his self-possession, and pushed him from him haughtily.

"Keep off, sir! I don't need the assistance of one who would stab me to the heart."

"Father! father! you are cruel. You know I would rather die than offend you," cried the warm-hearted boy.

"Then prove it," said the other, never softening that hard, cold stare. "You have taken a course that would wound me mortally—ay! beyond the power of earth to heal. You know me sufficiently to be aware that the two very offences you have confessed to are the bitterest affronts I could be offered in this world. You know also that I never forgive—never, though one word of forgiveness to an enemy could purchase me an eternity of happiness. One course alone remains for you, which, if you value me, you will adopt. Promise me to give up this hateful conspiracy, and retract your pledges of support to Captain Colthurst."

"Oh! anything but that," cried Charlie, eagerly.

"*Nothing* but that," was the stern response.

"Then come what will, that shall never be," almost

shouted the son, his eyes gleaming with enthusiastic resolution.

"Enough, sir," said the old man, with uncontrolled rage; "you have added the last bitterness to my cup of woes. You are no longer heir to Glengarra."

"But at least hear me, father."

"I have heard enough, sir."

"Nay, but you've heard nothing from me," cried the young man, determinedly. "You *must* hear me!"

"*Must!*" roared his father, his haughty lip curling.

"Yes, father, *must*," repeated Charlie, emphatically. "I don't much value the heirship of Glengarra. I am, thank God, both able and willing to carve out my own way in this world; but I shrink from the ignominy of being thought ungrateful to you—you to whom I owe everything, even my very life. I repel the foul charge, and in justice you must hear me while I try to justify myself. God only knows how sincerely I regret that our sympathies are so far apart; but between domestic and political obedience I must draw a line of distinction; and father though you are, I must claim for myself the liberty to think and act as I please in the political world."

"Even when it breaks a father's heart," broke in Mr. O'Hara, impatiently.

"The alternative is a dreadful one, but the call of duty smothers the loudest cry of affection. And, to my mind, duty makes what you consider crimes illustrious virtues. Need an Irishman make excuses to another for being what is termed a United Irishman? If so, then, the very necessity for such an excuse would be ample justification, for it would show how terribly this wretched land needs redress, when her own children are foremost to continue her subjection. But look around you, and every prospect, every ruined home, and every broken heart, must plead for me. What have I seen in my own day but a land speeding swiftly to destruction—ignorance and vice encouraged, because they destroy a noble nation—peasantry starving, maddened, aimless—corruption eating into the bowels of the State on one side, and misery sucking her very life-blood on the other—while over all this seething hell gloats a heartless spendthrift aristocracy, the stuffed effigies of a race of alien despots, the type of their ancestors, save in bravery and honor. Who says this mortifying canker must not be plucked out, root and branch? Who, that Ireland could not be, and should not be, as well as England, endowed with the mighty gift of incorruptible nationality?"

"Heavens! what a mass of infidel teaching!" cried the old man, almost involuntarily.

"Well, I will not pain you by pursuing the subject," said O'Hara, in a calmer tone. "Those feelings may be stupid, boyish, wicked—anything you like—but they are pure, and I feel proud of the opportunity of proving that they are sincere. As to my support of Captain Colthurst, I should only pain you, I fear, by justifying myself. I will not dwell upon the fact that he is an Irishman, while Lord Crabshawe is a mongrel—that he *knows* the people, while Lord Crabshawe *hates* them—that he is a *man*, while Lord Crabshawe is an *ass*. But on this alone I rest my defence—he has saved Milly—and gratitude alone would make me give my life for him."

"I have listened to you, sir," said Mr. O'Hara, his features now again composed into unpitying harshness—"I have listened to you with patience, and you have only convinced me the more how irretrievably you have lost my confidence. Let life teach you the wickedness of your prejudices against everything good and noble: you are now at liberty to satiate yourself with the smiles of the rabble you are so fond of."

"Let us part in peace, father," interrupted the young man, a flush of anger crimsoning his cheek, "I'm fond of no rabble, but of a confiding, a betrayed, and a glorious people."

"To the deepest hell, sir, with your vulgar distinctions," shouted his father, in ungovernable rage. "Don't beard me with them here. They *are* a rabble—a despicable, brutal rabble."

"You are my father, sir, or I would answer you," said O'Hara, suppressing his anger, with a mighty effort; "but I can hear no more of this. *My* resolution is taken. Is yours?"

"Undoubtedly," thundered the father. "You leave my house this night, and for ever."

"Be it so," said O'Hara, firmly. "I hope you will one day see how you have wronged us both."

And, without another word, father and son parted—parted as two whose paths were separate forevermore.

Mick Hoolohan was still there when Charles O'Hara descended to the foot of the stairs. The faithful fellow saw, as if by instinct, that some great sorrow had come upon his young master, and he followed him silently out into the garden until he rested himself in a shady arbor, when, with all the touching sincerity of a simple soul, he asked him what had happened.

Charmed with the feeling of attachment and love that beamed in every line of the poor fellow's face, O'Hara informed him, simply and sadly, of what had just passed between himself and his father.

As he finished, he could see the big tears gathering in that rough man's eye, and they clasped each other's hands—master and man—by an affectionate impulse that neither could resist.

"An' so you'll have to lave the ould place, Masther Charles!" said Mick, in a tone of touching sadness.

"Yes, Mick, I'll leave in a couple of hours."

"Masther Charles"—began the faithful fellow, raising his eyes as if hesitatingly.

"Well, Mick?"

"Masther Charles—av coorse, I'll go wid you!"

"Ten thousand thanks, Mick," cried O'Hara, again grasping his hand warmly, "but you know it is useless—I've not a farthing in the world."

"A farthin', Masther Charles!" cried the poor fellow reproachfully. "You don't think 'tis goin' to make money out av you I'd be? Begor, I haven't a half farthin' myself," he added gaily, " an' yet I've a notion I won't be widout my dinner."

"Well, then, if you wish it, come, Mick. All I can say is, you'll have a share of what's going, whether it's in a palace or a cabin."

"That's as it should be, Masther Charles," cried Mick, joyfully. "The divil a happier man than myself from this to the Giant's Causeway this moment. For though you're to the fore yourself, bad luck to me if I wudn't sooner be atin praties wid one o'yer family than pickin' a roast turkey wid the Lor' Liftenant o' the land."

"Well, then, here's a mission for you. Go find Mr. Inkston immediately, and tell him that I want to see him particularly here."

He was gone before the order was given, and had returned before ten minutes with the reply.

Mr. Inkston was unwell, and he should decline to see Mr. O'Hara.

Here, then, was the climax of this bewildering maze of events!

O'Hara dismissed his attendant to make the few preparations necessary for his journey. Then he threw himself on one of the rustic benches, and reflected.

What a tangled mysterious web had been woven

round his life in one short hour! This morning he had been a boy, in all the flush and buoyant ardor of youth—stranger to care—child of rosy hope and blooming life. Now he was an outcast from his home—alone in a wide, wide world—hedged in by the dark battalions of care—affections uprooted—associations rudely snapped—all, all the brilliant promise of a life smeared over with hideous blots—everything commingled in a world of chaos.

And all—why? Canvass it as he would, the answer did not supply itself. True, the vapory suspicions that had hovered round Inkston, as round some frowning hill, now rose in thick veils of mist. But they served only to thicken the mystery.

Inkston had betrayed him—foully, cruelly, inexplicably. But why? That generous heart revolted at any explanation that offered itself, for still did the holy bond of friendship soften all his darker thoughts. Inkston was not bad! He could never persuade himself that he was. But he had refused to see him—surely not through fear, for Inkston was no coward—and yet—and yet——

But speculation only led him into darker doubts, and he turned from it in dismay—turned to the spirit voices that kept whispering "it is fate"—and boldly shaking off every feeling of resentment, he girded himself for that struggle with the world which was now so imminent upon him.

To undo what had happened, he felt to be impossible—yet he looked back to it without a vengeful thought—even of Inkston—he could not hate him—like a spell his fatal influence coiled itself round that young heart.

And the tide of youthful life again surged up to his bosom, and with that mighty shield *mens conscia recti*, he faced the world with confidence, if not with hope.

While engaged in such thoughts, the fair form of a

girl had crept up beside him, and he was still deep in the warm embrace of his sister, who, as she pressed him to her heart, murmured, "Charlie, papa has told me all."

Oh! the exquisite agony and the burning pleasure of that parting—the sundering of two hearts that had grown like twin flowers from the sunny days of childhood! There in that garden, now robed in sympathetic wintriness, they had lisped each other's names in infancy; beyond, in that dear familiar lawn, now so woful and lonely, they had echoed the ring of their youthful laughter. And now—strong man and lovely girl—they were to break, perhaps for ever, those ties so deliciously woven. No wonder that tears should run from cheek to cheek, and that all the sweet weakness of woman should replace the old nervous bravery of Milly.

But why prolong the scene of sadness? They parted at last, with the mutual confidence that Providence would one day undo the mysterious chains that prisoned their happiness. Faithful to that inner prompting which still whispered that Inkston was no villain, O'Hara religiously refused to disclose, even to Milly, the author of all this ruin and disaster. He asked her to believe with himself that it was some wise dispensation of the Almighty, and that some day or other the clouds overhanging their lives would break in a blaze of sunny happiness.

If he had courage to confront ill-fortune, so had she—there was, in fact, something soothing to her nature in this sudden reaction from the gay levity of the coquette to the holy reflection of the woman.

Before they parted she had slipped into his hand a weighty purse of gold, wrung by her entreaties from their stern father.

Then, with one last embrace and trustful whisper, they said farewell!

CHAPTER IX.

CAPTAIN CROFTS' LITTLE GAME.

His strong heart bowed, not broken, by the disasters that had come so heavily upon him, Charles O'Hara turned from the home of his boyhood—the scene of all his purest and most elysian delights—the tender ties that a practical world had not yet unwound from his heart—and entered on the cold world of realities and sorrows.

His thoughts were as yet too overpowered by recent events to allow of provision for the future. His promise to Captain Colthurst determined him on visiting his friends in the first instance—beyond that, his plans were as yet unformed.

The gravity of the situation did not appear to weigh as heavily on his faithful henchman, who trotted down the avenue with their modest baggage, singing "Johnny the Bog-trotter," in a tone of more than ordinary hilarity.

As they reached the front gate, Frank Inkston's taciturn servant, James, issued from a neighboring copse, and placed himself full in their path.

With lightning rapidity, Mick's ditty ceased, and an unmistakable look of mischief replaced his good-humored smile. He glared at the unfortunate valet with the ferocity of a tiger, and then, leaping from the saddle, he collared him round the neck in an iron grasp, and swung him round and round until the poor wretch's face became a livid green.

"In God's name what do you mean, man?" cried O'Hara springing from his horse, and extricating the victim with the greatest difficulty.

"Ha! bad luck to the blackguard," growled Mick, in savage disappointment. "'Tis roasted be a slow fire he ought to be. Wait a while, Beelzeebub," he added, shaking his fist fiercely at his enemy; "I'll meet you yet for it, yourself an' your black thief of a masther."

"Silence, Mick," said O'Hara, sternly; then turning to the valet, "Do you want anything with me?"

The imperturbable James, who, throughout this noisy episode, had preserved a dogged and inconstruable silence, now drew forth from his breast a carefully-folded note, and having handed it to O'Hara, disappeared as noiselessly as he had come.

As O'Hara conjectured, the note was from Inkston, and, read by the light of what had just happened, appeared to O'Hara more incomprehensible still than his treachery. It ran thus:—

"Mr O'Hara,—(I cannot now call you by any more affectionate title) I cannot suffer you to go, without reminding you of your promise when I came to Glengarra, that you would not judge me harshly without hearing me. I dare not now see you or explain myself. One day the mystery will be cleared up. I am myself as great a sufferer as you. I am at once your deadly enemy and your fastest friend. It is useless for you now to seek to dive into my secret. We shall meet again. Frank Inkston."

Here was then the very perfection of entanglement and mystery—a net woven with tripled intricacy—a hideous prison of doubt where the very air was laden with inscrutable vapors.

Blindly, madly, he sought to unravel its perplexity—

an enemy and yet a friend—an avowed and dastardly traitor, and yet arrayed in the garb of one of destiny's martyrs!

Nor would his speculations have been helped, could he have dived into that sad chamber where the author of all his woes sat listening to his valet's recital of how his message had been received. For that noble form, that haggard face and anguished countenance, told not of the successful villain, but rather of one whose sufferings were beyond human ken.

But such communion was impossible. Charles O'Hara only knew that he knew nothing, and finding himself powerless to redeem his insolence, he resigned himself after a time to the mystery he could not penetrate.

The ride to Kilfinane Cottage, the residence of Captain Colthurst, was a long one, and, the air being sharp and breezy, O'Hara felt his spirits revive as the miles flew by. Mick's overflowing humor, too, came to his rescue, and the two rattled along merrily enough over the rough, zigzag road.

When they arrived at the cottage—a pretty, rose-trained little snuggery—it was already becoming dark, and they were astonished to find the door open, for Jack Colthurst had, notably, reason to scrutinize his visitors. Still more was O'Hara surprised, as he entered the hall, to hear the sounds of a desperate struggle going on inside.

Instinctively he divined the cause, and rushed to the little parlor, whence the crash and tumult of the strife proceeded.

He took in "the situation" at a glance. Three men, in the costume of comfortable farmers, were engaged in a violent struggle with Captain Colthurst. One of them had been felled to the ground, and lay a senseless heap among the combatants. The captain had seized one of the others by the throat, and was making a desperate effort to get him under, while with the other hand he wielded a huge fire-tongs, with which he aimed rapid lunges against his third assailant. The latter was armed with a tremendous cudgel, and while evading skilfully the captain's fierce onslaughts, was himself only awaiting the opportunity to deal him a "clincher" with the shillelagh.

With a shout of triumph Colthurst hailed the advent of his friend. Tightening his clutch on his smaller foe, he abandoned the other for a moment, and aimed a smart blow of the tongs at his immediate victim, which, however, that individual skilfully evaded, striving, at the same time, with desperation, to wrest the weapon from his hands. His companion of the shillelagh, now assured that his opportunity had come, aimed a deadly blow at the captain's head, which would have most infallibly smashed it, but that O'Hara leaped promptly to the rescue, and whisking the shillelagh out of its owner's hands, held him at arms-length in a grip of iron.

This movement decided the fray. With simultaneous impulse the two frieze-coats saw that 'twas all up, and cried "quarter!" in all sincerity.

They were immediately released, and the two friends embraced with hearty pleasure.

"Here, now, gentlemen," said Colthurst, wiping the perspiration from his big brow, and smiling most blandly at his discomfited assailants, "you'll please to consider yourselves prisoners of war until after the election. I won't keep ye in as pleasant a place as my quarters would be in Clonmel gaol; but if ye don't object to bacon and cabbage, and the first vintage from this to Slievenamon, I think ye'll be very much obliged to me for your imprisonment. Here, Biddy," he cried to a ragged old woman that now made her appearance

at the door, "your good man will take good care that
these gentlemen don't leave Kilfinane till after the election.
For the present, boys, ye must have an extra big
glass of whiskey, for devil a cleverer or a braver set of
blackguards I ever met. Only for Mr. O'Hara ye'd
have me as sure as a gun. However, console yourselves
under the circumstances. I'll send my best compliments
to Mr. Markham, and tell him ye behaved as
gallantly as ever a hangman did."

There was really not a word of reproof or displeasure
in this pleasant speech, and the fellows themselves
seemed to be quite comforted after their disappointment.

"Begor, sir," says one, twisting his hat uneasily,
"'twasn't our fault that we didn't nab you. Shure, for
the matter o' that, there isn't a gintleman in Tipperary
I'd sooner lose my life for than yerself, an' 'tis proud I
am that I wasn't able to split your skull as I intinded.
But a fellow must do what he's ordhered, sir."

"Quite right," said the captain, complacently. "'Live
and let live' has been always a precept of mine, especially
in the matter of bum-bailiffs. But come, rout
up that lazy sprissaun in the corner there, and take
yourselves off to Biddy's quarters, and mark you!—no
attempt at escape, or by the powers! I'll have ye strung
up *instanter*."

"Niver fear, sir," said the fellows in unison, as they
hauled themselves and their insensible comrade out of
the room, "'tisn't often we get the chance of a couple
of days good feedin'."

"And now," cried Colthurst, with a jolly smile, as the
door closed on the bailiffs, "now I'm at liberty, at last,
to bid you welcome, and to ask how are you?"

"Methinks the interrogatory might come more properly
from me," said O'Hara, with a smile at the disordered

dress and perspiring brow of his friend. "Who are those friends of yours?"

"Oh! very good fellows in their way," said the captain. "They're members of a confraternity who honor me with the most courteous attentions. The rascals are bum-bailiffs, and came to execute some confounded decree that Markham of Clonmel has against me."

"Why, how comes that, Jack?" cried O'Hara; "Kilfinane Cottage has the reputation of being one of the strongest fortresses in Ireland when bailiffs are in the question. They tell sundry sad tales of your contempt for the king's writ."

"Well," said the captain, with an easy smile, "considering that there are some thirty-five such pieces of royal parchment hanging over my head this moment, I don't consider I've forfeited my reputation. But listen, and you'll agree with me that those fellows tried to play me a pretty trick. A quarter of an hour ago, Biddy came to tell me that three men outside the front gate wanted to see me. 'Are they like bailiffs, Biddy?' says I. 'Well, sir,' says she, 'they're too comfortable-lookin' for anything else.' 'Then throw a kettle of boiling water on them, Biddy,' I said, and resigned myself again to my *otium cum dig.*, confident that they would not be able to penetrate to the door. But Biddy returned in a minute. 'I gev it to 'em, bilin', sir,' says she, 'but the divil wouldn't make 'em go. They says they're the canvassers from Killenaule, and that they've great news for you about th' election.' 'Thunder-an'-turf! Biddy,' cried I, 'you've done it nicely—you've scalded my best supporters!' I rushed to the gate—the ruffians looked so honest in their big frieze coats that I received them with open arms. The old story of Troy repeated—the enemy admitted *intra mœnia.* They talked like parrots of my chances round Killenaule. I talked like Grat-

tan of what I'd do for Ireland! What with a couple of
glasses of whiskey and a song, we were becoming patri-
otically jolly, when bang! I got a blow of a shillelagh
right in the back of the head. Instantly I smelt powder,
and had barely time to seize the tongs when the whole
three of them came at me like a pack of wolves. A smart
tip on the head sent one of them to temporary oblivion;
but the other blackguards had skulls as hard as rocks,
and they were so well able to use their shillelaghs, that
I'd probably be in kingdom come by this time but for
your timely aid!"

"A most tragic tale," remarked O'Hara, with a hearty
laugh. "But where is Miss Colthurst? I hope she
hasn't heard anything of this?"

"I may bless my stars for it, my boy—she's gone over
to see Miss Ryan, the priest's sister. I wouldn't wish
for a thousand pounds to have her here. Poor Lucy!
she is not able to appreciate these little incidents. She
thinks as much of a broken bone, I declare, as if she
had not been with me side-by-side among the bloodiest
scenes of the Revolution."

"It's her love for you, Jack," said O'Hara, with something like a sigh. "Little wonder that she doesn't like
your being perpetually engaged in this struggle with the
law. It must be an awful life."

"Not at all, my dear boy," replied Colthurst cheerfully." "Plenty of excitement, and scarcely a bit of
danger—precisely what I like. Here I am, provisioned
and garrisoned as in a little fortress of my own; there's
something grand in the thought that a fellow might be
called on to fight for his life at ten minutes notice."

"Well, well, it might be so. But how in the name of
wonder can you get through the election with all these
writs hanging over you?"

"Simply by making them afraid of me, Charlie,"
7

said Colthurst, determinedly. "If they won't have peace, I'll give them war—ay, war to their heart's content. But, speaking of war and of the election, reminds me—you wouldn't think it!—I've got a challenge to-day from Lord Crabshawe."

"From Lord Crabshawe!" exclaimed O'Hara, in unfeigned surprise. "In heaven's name, why?"

"Oh! a couple of words we had yesterday."

"But are you serious? Surely, Lord Crabshawe doesn't mean to fight?"

"So 'twould seem, faith. Not only was his message insulting, but the fellow that brought it—that fellow Crofts—got so impudent, that I had to throw him out through the front window."

"And you really think he'll fight?"

"I don't know, faith. It struck me as rather odd, though, that the challenge had hardly come when those bailiff fellows attempted to get me out of the way. That looks like treachery. If I thought 'twas Crabshawe was at the bottom of this Markham business, upon my honor, I'd be inclined to horsewhip him within an inch of his life."

"When did he appoint to meet you?"

"To-morrow morning at the Grange. I suppose I may count on you as my second?"

"Decidedly. But, of course, you won't shoot the poor fool?"

"Oh! certainly not; I want to give him a decent beating on the hustings."

"What if this duel business should also be a snare?"

"True; that Crofts is ruffian enough to hang his father and preach a lecture on filial affection afterwards. But he'd better not try that game with me. No, Charlie, we'll go there, at all events."

"With all my heart," said O'Hara — "the more especially as I have no other engagement."

The bitterness of his tone startled the captain, and now marking for the first time his friend's altered manner, he earnestly inquired the cause.

In a few unadorned sentences O'Hara narrated what had passed between himself and his father, and explained his altered circumstances.

Colthurst heard him with all the manly affection of the real friend.

"And all for me, my dear friend," he cried, wringing O'Hara's hand warmly.

"All for duty, Jack," cried O'Hara, proudly.

"Charlie, you're a man, every inch of you," exclaimed Colthurst, in genuine admiration. "But, after all, I am selfish enough to be satisfied with what has happened. Now we may be really friends, meeting on an equal footing, and equally circumscribed in our incomes."

"Then seal the compact, Jack," cried O'Hara, warmly. "We're *friends* henceforth."

"*In sæcula sæculorum*, my boy," replied Jack, with an excruciating shake of the hand. "But a truce to our pledges. Here comes Lucy."

CHAPTER X.

LUCY COLTHURST.

The history of the Colthurst family was a chequered and eventful one, teeming with events at which we can only briefly glance. Like many others of the older Irish houses, its head had been involved in the intrigues attending the struggles of the young Pretender. Like many others, too, on the failure of that prince's rebellion, the elder Colthurst had to fly to France, and carried over with him his family, consisting of a son and daughter, in addition to a wife, a Frenchwoman by birth. They had lived in comparative affluence at the court of the French monarch until the outbreak of the Revolution, when, amid all the turbulent fury of that sanguinary time, Mr. Colthurst fell a victim to his royalist connection, and expired under the guillotine a few days after his royal patron. Strange to say, his son, heedless of this terrible example, plunged headlong into the revolutionary maelstrom. He joined the French army while yet a boy, and, through the troublous days of the early revolution, followed the disastrous banner of the Republic over many a hard-fought field in Alsace. On the plains of Valmy and Fleurus the gallant young soldier won clustering laurels, and for his surpassing bravery in the subsequent campaign he received from the hands of Pichegru himself the commission of captain in the noble corps which he had followed over many a field of fame. But his military career was nipped in the bud when he received the intelligence that his mother, overwhelmed by the shock of her husband's death, had succumbed to a lingering disease, and that his sister Lucy was thus left alone and friendless amid the noisy turmoil of Paris.

He immediately, though with deep regret, renounced the career that was opening up to him such an exciting future, and repaired to the capital. The influence of a powerful friend at the court of King George procured the revocation of the attainder against the remnant of his father's property, and all employment save the military being then paralyzed in France, he abandoned the country of his adoption, and sailed for Ireland with his sister, where he settled down with resignation, if with reluctance, to the humdrum life of an Irish country gentleman.

A dashing figure, a brave hand, and a warm heart might have, *cæteris paribus*, made Jack Colthurst prince of his fellows. But, like all the other children of the Republic—their principles born in carnage and baptized in blood, and hallowed by a sort of barbarous glory, the magnificence of slaughter—his very soul had been saturated with the revolutionary contagion. The memories of the heroic gallantry of the citizen soldiers with whom he had fought, of the rude splendor of their victories, and the excitement of their disasters, were still present to his mind as though he were storming the Bastile to the stern crash of the "Marseillaise." For love of his sister, he curbed all his more martial inclinations, and being naturally of an accommodating disposition, applied himself to live as contentedly as he might amid his aristocratic compeers. But the magic words "Liberty, Equality, and Fraternity," so often inscribed on the gonfalon of despotism and hate, were to him ever full of a sublime humanitarianism, which he felt it a duty to propagate.

Transferred abruptly from the delusive socialism and popular license to which France had committed herself, to the darkness and feudalism of Ireland's most feudal county, he could ill restrain the thoughts which the contrast suggested.

We will not be accused of misrepresentation or partiality when we say that the state of Tipperary at the end of the last century was such as to strike wonder and dismay into the citizen of a free land. Unchanged in any material way by the influences that had moulded Europe into comparative civilization, Ireland retained the most barbarous forms of feudalism without any of those sympathies that made feudalism tolerable. Society grouped into two rude and hostile classes. On one side, a nation of serfs embruted by ignorance, steeled by oppression, vilely complaisant where they could not be deadly foes, sullenly hating what they did not dare to resist, powerless to rise from the slough of despond, powerful only to plunge deeper into despair, and to explore further depths of degradation. On the other side, an oligarchy, alien in blood, in sympathy, and thought; barbarously squalid or magnificent beggars, if they were not griping and unscrupulous misers; dependent for power on the destruction of the people; accepting their advances with freezing suspicion, or punishing their hatred with unsparing severity. Such was the sad spectacle of Ireland's social degradation, such the secret of the dire rapidity with which she was hurrying to a deserved destruction. We need not here examine causes fraught with memories of bitterness and shame to both sides. Thank heaven! the sickening sight has been swept away in our own days, and in the bright light of education and truth the hidden sympathies between class and class, so long sundered by faults on all sides, are blending again in divinest concord.

But, in the days of which we write, what is now but an evil tradition, or, at worst, an exceptional disgrace, was everywhere in Ireland the rule. and nowhere so unfortunately so as in Tipperary.

Fresh from republican France, and full of its shadowy notions of the infallibility of the people, Captain Colthurst marked all these disorders and miseries that harried the land, and, perhaps too hastily, came to the conclusion that the people were all right, and that the landlords were all wrong. He saw only that the one were slaves, and the other tyrants; and, by nature fearless as he was honest and uncompromising, he lost no opportunity of divulging his views, in season and out of season, to his aristocratic compeers.

It may easily be supposed that ideas so foreign to all the rights of property and prescription, aroused the utmost jealousy among a class, who, ordinarily combined to resist and chastise every symptom of popular discontent, were now especially united against that spirit of equality and democracy whose trump had already thundered through the uttermost limits of Europe. Proceeding from one of their own body, they regarded them as still more dangerous—one, moreover, who had drunk in the doctrines of socialism at their very fount and source, and who, by his lavish extravagance and kindly qualities, had rallied the herd into a disposition to hearken to his apostolicism.

We have deemed it important to trace so far the causes of Captain Colthurst's estrangement from the territorial lords of his neighborhood, considering that they may also give us a clue to the motives that led him to embark in the wild struggle for the representation of the county against the combined phalanx and the mighty interests enlisted against him.

But, whatever his political or social views, we have

seen enough of Captain Colthurst to know, that, with true soldierly instinct, his brimming spirits ever befriended him, and that, however bitter the antipathy of his associates, he managed to live as pleasantly and enjoy himself as thoroughly as if he were still winning glory on the battlefields of Germany among his old group of jolly comrades. It is needless to add that a character so formed was an idol with the mob, and an idol all the more that his inconsiderate hospitality had scattered to the winds the small remnant of his patrimony.

Never did nature, in all her arbitrary affection for grotesquerie, throw together two souls more radically different and yet more subtly in sympathy than Captain Colthurst and his sister Lucy. He was the MAN in every line of his face, in every motion of his mind, in every drop of blood that swelled through his veins. She was the WOMAN of poetry's chastest dream, the creature of light, the shape of loveliness, the heart of truth and purity. Amid the din and roar of conflict, the martial heraldry of death, the unprisoned riot of the soldier's gaiety, was his congenial sphere; his soul still revelled in the grim banquet-halls of glory, his spirit bent not to the grave whisperings of thought. She was, on the contrary, the very perfection of womanliness, sharing that delicious weakness, that passionate, almost romantic tenderness, and that ineffable sense of truthfulness for which the fairest of her sex have been prized. Shrinking from the harsh sounds of strife or of boisterous mirth, in which her brother delighted, she especially loved every scene of peaceful happiness or poetic beauty. Perhaps the memory of the bleeding victim on the Place Louis Quatorze, and the no less suffering soul that had breathed out its life in her arms, still shadowed the existence of Lucy Colthurst, and rendered hateful to her every memento of that blood-stained time.

Yet with all these jarring inconsistencies of disposition, brother and sister never loved one another with a love more pure or more devoted than did they. Lucy's gentle nature clung round that great stalwart soldier as a vine might round an oak; and he returned the affection with a sort of enraptured adoration. If she blamed him for his recklessness, or chided him for his contempt of danger, he assuaged her by his generous devotion, and by his ready obedience to her every wish.

In person, Lucy Colthurst was rather exquisitely than dazzlingly beautiful. The artist would have stopped to study her perfection, while the less critical passed on to some more *éclatante* picture. Hers was the pure and luscious beauty of nature, unadorned by the world's beautifying arts. Her figure was somewhat delicately slender, though perfectly proportioned. Her face—soft and clearly outlined—was just pale and transparent enough to give it a preternaturally *spirituel* hue, while the faint under-color of pink, ever varying with the heightened rose of the most guileless innocence, was there to give her woman's loveliest and most potent charm. Lips of the reddest coral, and wavy tresses of that sweet shade of browning auburn, in which the sunlight loves to nestle, gave lustre to a face whose primal beauty yet was the magic enchantment of her eyes. They might have been hazel, or a deeper brown, in different lights, but above every effect of color was the liquid sea of light in which they seemed to be bathed, and which imparted to the fair girl all that wealth of poetic idealism, and all that look of trusting fondness which a ripe age had not yet developed into burning love.

Charles O'Hara had known Lucy Colthurst since she

left France, and a couple of years had barely passed since they played together in the unordered familiarity of children. Yet he was scarcely prepared for the great change even the short time since their last meeting had made in his old playmate. The girl was fast budding into the woman; the mantling charms, before hidden under the veil of childhood, were fast flushing into full life, and instead of the pretty thoughtful child, he found himself standing with awe and constraint before a beautiful woman.

Did she also mark in that first rapid glance a something nobler and more manly than rosy-cheeked little Charlie could boast? Perhaps the surprise was mutual, for both blushed most perceptibly, and their greeting was formal enough to set Jack Colthurst staring and thinking why it was so.

But the embarrassment was only momentary. Their store of mutual reminiscences, the whole history of their lives, in which all of them felt interest, soon kindled their converse into the old warmth. But such *reunions*, agreeable as they may be to those immediately interested, are devoid of attraction to the ordinary reader, and we cannot here transcribe them. With her natural aversion to society, Lucy mingled little in the rude life around her, and applied herself more to the cultivation of those arts that softened her many solitary hours. She could, therefore, discourse on most subjects with a power beyond that of the general class of women of the time, and, moreover, adorned her conversation with a sort of romantic halo that lent it, perhaps, its most powerful charm.

"I have urged Jack, in vain, Mr. O'Hara," she said with a sigh, "to give up this foolish project of contesting the county. I abhor those perpetual scenes of danger. But Jack seems so fond of it that I fear he will never listen to what he calls my foolish fears. If you joined me, Mr. O'Hara, perhaps my remonstrances would not be so barren."

"Alas! where *such* entreaty fails, persuasion is surely impossible," said O'Hara, gallantly.

"Yes; that's a very fine speech," remarked Jack, in his most off-hand tone, "but don't believe a word of it, Lucy. The rascal himself is my conducting agent."

"Well, if that be so, it's some consolation," said Miss Colthurst, with a smile. "Mr. O'Hara is not likely to fight as many duels as you are before the election."

"Faith, then, I can tell you he's no new hand at that same," cried Colthurst, laughing; "I wouldn't be surprised if he was making arrangements this moment for one to-morrow morning."

"If I am, it's not likely you're to be out of the pie," laughed O'Hara. "But in all seriousness, Miss Colthurst, I'm afraid Jack has betrayed me. I must plead guilty to being an ally of his in this electoral campaign."

"But how could you, too, be so infatuated?" asked she, sadly. "You must surely see the odds that are against him. You must be aware that the very name of democrat is enough to brand him as a rebel, and to make him a mark for the secret vengeance of every coward who fears to meet him openly."

"Now, Lucy," cried her brother, kissing her brow, endearingly, "you are the dearest, loveliest little pet in the world, and if 't was going to buy a new hat or take a wife I was, I'd take your advice as if 't was one of the ten commandments; but, as I often told you, you're only a child yet in politics and war."

"Well, maybe so, Jack," said Lucy, smiling; "but still I'd like to know why."

"Begor, as to that," cried the captain, bluntly, "I never had a taste for long speeches. It's a rule in the army, you know—never ask the why nor the wherefore. But Charlie will be my advocate; give us one or two out of the thousand reasons why 't is necessary to wallop those Sassenachs."

"The fact that you've determined on walloping them would, I fancy, be pretext enough," said O'Hara, with a smile. "But I'm sure it's her affections, not her convictions, that are troubling Miss Colthurst. The heaped miseries of this very neighborhood, of which, if report speak truly, she is no unsympathetic witness, call for redress in tones of thunder."

"Alas! yes!" assented Miss Colthurst, her long eyelashes drooping sadly. "It is too true that misery has branded '*Mine*' on the very homes and hearts of our poor people."

"The eloquent witnesses of disaster cross our path at every step," he continued; "a noble and a generous race, thinned by oppression where they are not decimated by famine—degraded with vicious indulgence, if they are not stricken with despair—and not a hand raised to avert their doom—not one to arrest the fatal march of the destroyer. Yes! one—one *has* arisen—from end to end of Ireland already we hear the ominous mutterings of his teachings—one gleam of hope is faintly bursting through this thick darkness of ages—and if the awakening—ay! if 't were even the Revolution in its deadliest shape—be accomplished, we may yet hope for the happiness of the Irish race. Your brother's victory—even his defeat—would be an immense stride towards that consummation. Surely, you will rather buoy him up with your smiles than discourage him by your disapproval?"

"Oh! yes," exclaimed Miss Colthurst, to whose ductile soul the speaker had communicated some of his rather hot enthusiasm; "you have indeed placed it in a different light. Yet my heart misgives me as to the result. Poor Jack! I would trust him against a whole regiment, one by one; but even *he* cannot compass impossibilities. Human bravery has no armor against the base treachery of these petty tyrants."

"A brave heart is proof against the artifices of the whole world," cried O'Hara. "And brave hearts in thousands will rally round the man who first cries 'God save the people!'"

"You have shamed me from my doubts," she cried, at last yielding to the enthusiasm of the moment. "I make the sacrifice willingly, proudly. The cause must be a noble one that would enlist such advocacy."

"It shall be all the nobler for your kind blessing," cried O'Hara, with flushed cheek.

"Well," deliberately commenced the captain, who had listened to this passage in silent amazement, "'tis only one other proof of the superiority of mind over matter; for if I had a whole train of metaphysical siege-guns hammering at Lucy, they wouldn't be half so effective as those couple of sentences of yours."

Lucy blushed, and O'Hara felt a thrilling sort of pleasure that he had never experienced before.

"But now that the poetic part is over," continued the captain, "perhaps ye'd leave a plain-spoken man to inform ye that there's no need for a bit of fuss about the matter, because it is as sure as that there's a tail on a horse that I'll be M. P. for Tipperary by the end of the week. But now that you've been talking of all the danger that's before *me*, I think 'tis only fair to inform Lucy of the pleasant predicament your're in yourself this moment," and before O'Hara could stop him he had related the entire story of his difference with his father.

Lucy listened with absorbing interest. She was

amazed and stunned by the intelligence, and her momentary change of color betrayed her anxious attention to the tale. In words of most soothing sympathy she then commiserated him on what had happened, and with womanly solicitude questioned him as to his plans for the future.

"By Jove! I was forgetting to ask you all about that, my boy," cried the captain. "What do you intend to do?"

"Oh! anything—nothing," said O'Hara, confusedly. "The fact is, I've not had time to think on the matter. I'll go to Dublin first, at any rate."

"But of course you'll stay with us for the present—until after the election, at least," said Colthurst. "You know I could never do without you during the contest, for you're a host in yourself. After that 'twill be time enough to be discussing what you'll do. I won't promise you all the luxuries of Glengarra, but if *cead mille failthe* will supply the deficiencies, we'll make you as happy as the days are long."

"Let me add my strongest entreaties, Mr. O'Hara," said Lucy.

As she spoke, their eyes met for the first time in a glance of unspeakable ecstasy.

"I'll decidedly remain," said O'Hara, and he felt his soul afire with a new passion.

The first breathings of love

CHAPTER XI.

ELECTIONEERING JOYS.

Miss Colthurst did not overrate the arduous struggle in which her brother had been engaged. Strange as it may appear at this distance of time, when political freedom is pushing its branches everywhere, the attempt might be considered little short of madness.

Caricaturists have told funny things of the lower order of Irishmen in the last century, and have depicted them as a set of light-hearted dare-devils, galloping on to perdition to the tune of "Paddy Go Easy," and on the most amicable terms with their body-guard of misfortunes. For Tipperary, at all events, the picture is overdrawn. Serfdom, with its train of accompanying evils, paralyzed every noble prompting of the peasantry. Long ages of unvarying calamity, the heritage of their race and nation, had made many of them passive slaves, wallowing in the *abandon* of despair and abasement. Others—and they were numerous—they had driven to the shelter of disastrous conspiracy and murderous combination. The massive frames, the giant limbs, and virile sinews of their mingled parentage, still marked those dwellers in the Golden Vein; but their hearts were crushed or despairingly defiant, their spirits trodden out, their homes brinked with ruin, the very idea of liberty reduced to a distant phantom.

Under the shifting countenance of patriotism the more daring found a refuge in lawlessness, and, pressed round with dangers, invoked "the wild justice of revenge" to parry that equally terrible retaliation farcically termed justice. In those dark retreats of ignorance and crime Freedom lost all its holier significance, and stood simply for the vague conception of Revenge.

The brief era of the Volunteers and Grattan's inspired eloquence penetrated for a time the dense abodes of ignorance. The spectacle of a free nation filled with enthusiasm a land long nursed in contention. A new light was poured on the dark waters, pierced their deepest recesses with lustrous ray, and then fled away, alas! like a beauteous dream.

But now in its orbit sprung up a fiercer fire. The smooth-toned voice of Revolution whispered words of encouragement. They fell gratefully on hearts long seared with disaster; and the perilous daring of the few merged in the ominous awakening of the many.

Wolfe Tone and his associates had breathed the spirit of the French republicans into the Irish masses. The society of United Irishmen he had formed was steadily, if slowly, asserting its power; and for the first time since the misty days of "the Blackbird," the Irish people dared to array themselves against their masters.

To Captain Colthurst's lot fell the first open assertion of this new and powerful spirit. He was, perhaps, best fitted for the post by his popularity and associations; but even he himself scarcely realized the difficulty of his position. His allies were wavering, dejected, intractable; the lawless license of some had to be checked—the lingering slavishness of others hurried away. Heaven only knew whether a race accustomed to subjection would not shrink from open desertion of their masters; or worse, whether they would not rush into the opposite extreme of disorder. To the feeble and ill-understood promptings of liberty were opposed every consideration of interest or of terror. The ruling classes were banded together to a man. They wielded a power that had never yet been resisted. The voters were their serfs—wealth and *prestige* their allies. At their beck thousands of homes might be levelled; a ruthless and an alien soldiery were at their service to trample out where self-interest failed to conciliate. On the popular side were enthusiasm, misery, poverty: on the aristocratic, all that could excite cupidity, or influence by terror.

As they sat over their wine, in Lucy's absence, Charles O'Hara, whom recent events had made graver and more calculating, rehearsed all those difficulties, and dwelt on the uncertainty of the issue.

But Colthurst laughed off his misgivings. He said he was aware of all the dangers of his position, but he did not think them insuperable. The enthusiasm of the people had been aroused to fever heat; the force of the secret organizations through the country was on his side; the enemy were not much prepared, and had not an idea of the extent of his strength; in short, with pluck and resolution, all might be carried at a dash. But he had one power in reserve, with which he hoped to overbear all opposition. The clergy were on his side. They were the great countervailing influence to that of the landlords. The prerogative of the one was as unlimited as the power of the other. Thousands would rather dare ruin at the hands of the landlords, than displeasure at those of the priests. Their spiritual influence was strengthened by their espousal of every popular cause, and by their education, which lifted them high above the intelligence of their unenlightened flock. With them, Colthurst counted on an easy victory, and O'Hara agreed with him that the prospect was not hopeless. That evening, so close on the election, was not a very quiet one for the Popular Candidate. An almost continuous stream of visitors, on the business of the election, were arriving at the little front gate, and were, after the usual scrutiny, admitted.

First came, splashed and travel-stained, a courier from near Carrick, a stalworth, earnest-looking peasant, having determination and honesty written on every line of his face. He looked disappointed at the result of his mission. The poor people of that neighborhood, he said, were heart and soul with the cause; but all of them had been subject to merciless coercion. One was threatened with eviction—another with a rise of rent— a third with deprival of some cherished privilege—if they should countenance the candidature of the Captain.

"The truth is, sir," said the courier, sadly, "the sowl is crushed out of 'em. But niver mind for that, we may manage it yit."

"How's that, Paddy?"

"They wouldn't mind bein' *forced* to vote right," said the other significantly. "There's a couple o' hundhrid bys out in that direction, an' if I can get 'em together on the day o' the pollin' *we* might do escort duty as well as the dhragoons."

"By Jove! you're a treasure, Paddy," cried Colthurst, with a laugh; "I give you an unlimited commission; only mind this—that you don't force any man who you don't know would vote for me if he had his own choice."

His next visitor was a fussy little man, the editor of the *Clonmel Slasher*, a revered figure in county society, and imbued with the most extravagant notions of the omnipotence of his print.

"I've done some little things for you in the last *Slasher*, captain," said the little man, with a self-satisfied snigger. "I *think* they'll have some effect. I suppose you saw them?"

"Oh! yes, capital," assented the captain, who had not laid his eyes on the *Slasher* at all.

"Ah!" continued the editor, in the same jubilant tone, "that little stroke about 'To be, or not to be,' wasn't it nicely put? It takes Shakespeare to knock up life into those people."

"Yes," drawled Colthurst, who was beginning to think the editor an insufferable bore.

"Pshaw! sir, only for the Press, tyranny would be without stay or check, as I remarked in the last *Slasher*. The *Bugle* is getting alarmed at what it terms our dangerous doctrines."

"Yes," put in Colthurst, in a rather impatient tone, "but is there anything particular that gives me the honor of this visit?"

"Well, just a trifle," said the editor, disconcerted at this check to his volubility: "you see, captain, it doesn't pay to be attacking Lord Crabshawe—and you know it's expensive to keep up a newspaper like the *Slasher*. I suppose you know that we have a little account against you for advertisements—a trifle, you know."

"Pshaw! it's that you're up to?" cried Colthurst—"yours is an advocacy of pounds, shillings, and pence. Well, sir, you must go to some better market."

"Oh! excuse me——"

"No excuses required, sir, I'm afraid we'll have to dispense with the services of the *Slasher* and its editor," and with most polite gestures he bowed the poor man to the door, through which he disappeared, with a secret vow for the captain's annihilation in the forthcoming *Slasher*.

The man of types had scarcely gone, when the well-known trot of Father Mat Ryan's pony on the gravel announced the arrival of the good old parish priest. Father Mat was one of the finest types of the Tipperary pastor of the old times. Though his hair was silvering, and an expression of mild benevolence was settling over his sternly moulded features, he still exhibited those qualities of nerve and sturdiness, so requisite at a time when the priest had to be militant in more than a spiritual sense.

His giant frame was unbent; an easy, good-natured smile was on his face; and in his hand he carried a riding-whip, which, betimes, was more than an ornament. The good man had spent almost his lifetime among his present parishioners, and in the quality of guardian, priest, and friend, had earned the affection of everyone who knew him. With Colthurst he had been on terms of the freest intimacy, having known his father previous to his departure for France; and many a night Kilfinane Cottage had echoed the mirth of the gallant soldier and the sterling minister.

The young men received him with all the respect and cordiality due to his character, and Mike Hoolohan busied himself in caring for the creature comforts of the pony.

Father Mat had come as usual to have a quiet chat, over a jug of punch, on the prospects of the election. It was evident that, despite his friendship for Colthurst, he had not thrown his influence unreservedly into the balance on the popular side.

"If you went in on more moderate grounds now, Jack," he said, "we'd move heaven and earth for you; but you see the Church cannot countenance the shedding of blood, and—*beeshay mor shin*—they say you have very questionable relations with Tone and his fellows. For my own part, I may tell you, I wouldn't be far sorry for *anything* that would better our present position, but then chances must be taken into account. The clergy can't risk being beaten, you know. However, if 'twas only for auld lang syne, Jack, and for your poor father's sake, I'm with you heart and soul, and I'll do all I can for you, with all the other priests. Count on me, at any rate, and I'll have two hundred votes for you, as sure as the sun is shining."

After the priest, came a tall country fellow, wrapped up mysteriously in a rude disguise, which, on being lifted, disclosed features of a ferocious and more than ordinarily sagacious character. This was " the Captain," an individual known and dreaded through all the surrounding country, as the director of one of those secret combinations which spread such terror and confusion among the loyal inhabitants. The man was really gifted with powers above his station. The incessant danger of death or torture made him reckless; and, backed by a band of spirits as dangerous as himself, he wielded no contemptible power for good or evil. But he had his ambition, too, and never cared to play second fiddle where he knew he was wanted. For the rest, a savage temper, and a reckless barbarity, completed his character as the very worst type of the lowest Irishman, steeled and debased by a life of misfortune.

Colthurst had accepted his alliance as a necessity, because the lower orders looked up to "the Captain" as the very incarnation of strength, and because his coercive power almost outweighted that of the landlords. But he too well knew what an unmanageable instrument he was pressing into his service.

The outlaw shuffled into his presence with an air of defiant equality, his blackened face and close-drawn cloak adding to the undesirableness of his appearance.

"Hallo! Joe," cried Colthurst, as he entered. "How fared it with you to-day?"

"Damnably, captain, damnably," muttered the fellow, in a dogged voice. "Haven't eaten a bit for forty-eight hours. Give's somethin' t'ate."

A plentiful repast was set before him, to which he did justice voraciously, varying the meal with deep draughts of unadulterated whiskey.

"You're in a blessed humor to-night, Joe," ventured Colthurst, when the fellow had gorged himself to his fullest capacity.

"No more I ought to be," grunted "the Captain"—"it isn't sittin' by a cozy fire I was all day."

"But how did you succeed with the Clonmel boys?"

"Succeed!" cried the other, contemptuously; "I always succeed. Fellows never make a rumpus when I've a loaded pistol to their ear."

"Rubbish!" muttered Colthurst, impatient of the fellow's overbearing insolence. "Will they be all at the nomination on Friday for me?"

"They will," was the surly response. "But I tell you what, Captain Colthurst, they won't go for king or counthry unless they get the dhrink. Small blame to 'em, nayther, for Lord Crabshawe is spindin' money in oceans. It won't do widout the dhrink, I tell you. A fellow's sperrits must be kep up."

"Then to the devil with them," cried Colthurst, angrily. "I'll be able to do without them. I mistake not if you have not spoiled them, for 'tisn't a week ago since they were all ready to follow me without either fee or reward. Tell every man Jack of them, that I won't spend a ha'penny, and that, if they're not men, I won't make them brutes."

"P'rhaps Lord Crabshawe wouldn't be so bowld," remarked "the Captain," with an insolent sneer.

"What! fellow, do you intend to threaten?" cried Colthurst in amazement. "Confound your impudence, you scoundrel."

"The bowldest man in Tipperary wouldn't repate that word," shouted the outlaw, his eyes blazing with passion. "Even *you* dare to call the Captain a scoundhrel again, an' I'll lave you dead on the flure."

As he spoke, he drew from his breast a huge horse-pistol, and levelled it with savage determination at Colthurst's head. With the quick instinct of one accustomed to danger, Colthurst leaped from his seat, and wrenching the pistol from the fellow's hand, pointed it to his forehead significantly.

"Fool!" he cried, laughingly, "to think you could frighten me with your cut-throat grimaces. Take your pistol, man, and keep a civil tongue in your head in future. After all, perhaps I was too hasty. Shake hands, Joe, and lets forget it."

The outlaw took the proffered hand, returned the pistol to his breast, and reseated himself gloomily.

"'Tis all right, captain," he muttered, as he seized his hat and again shrouded himself in his rough disguise. "'Tis all right," and with a savage frown on the friends, he left the room.

"That fellow is another enemy," exclaimed O'Hara, when "the Captain" had disappeared. "He looks a villain fit for anything."

"Pshaw! he is contemptible," said Colthurst, quietly. "'Twas a mistake to suppose 'tis by such wretches a good cause can be upheld."

"I fear this night's work won't better the situation."

"Never mind," cried the captain, hopefully. "You've heard only the skirmishing—wait till we come to the charge. Meanwhile let's not forget that I have to fight Lord Crabshawe to-morrow morning. If the fellow should happen to hit me, will you, Charlie, take my place towards Lucy?"

"Till death!" came the answer from O'Hara's heart.

CHAPTER XII.

CAUGHT IN THE TRAP.

The gray dawn of the morning saw Captain Colthurst and Charles O'Hara at the trysting-place in the Grange, appointed for the duel with Lord Crabshawe. They were chatting away the time with numerous experiences of former "meetings," and were discussing the duello in a style that would have shocked a humanitarian like Paley.

The time wore on, however, and the sun began to peep out over the bare hills, and, by frequent consultations with his watch, Colthurst began to perceive that the time fixed for the meeting was considerably exceeded. Another chat, and another look at the watch, told that a quarter of an hour more had passed.

They were beginning to feel uneasy—for punctuality is the prime of virtues with the duellist; and Colthurst himself was beginning to believe that Lord Crabshawe had slept on his warlike resolution, when Captain Crofts' portly figure hove in view.

The captain was alone, and his big flabby features were composed into an expression of ceremonious gravity.

"Captain Colthurst—Mr. O'Hara—how do you do?" was his salute, as he raised his hat with professional urbanity.

"Well, I thank you," said Colthurst, brusquely. "Your man's not up to time."

"He is, sir, in time to the minute," replied Crofts, in the same funereal tone, "but an unfortunate—in fact, I may say, a dreadful—accident has occurred"——

"What!" cried the friends together, "has anything happened Lord Crabshawe?"

Crofts shook his head with doleful gravity.

"Come with me," he whispered, sympathetically, "he's at the lodge on the hill above."

"My God! what has happened him?" demanded Colthurst, with real concern.

The captain shook his head again significantly.

"Come," said he, dramatically, and taking the arm of O'Hara, who was next him, he turned towards the lodge he had indicated.

His mysterious silence quite imposed on the young men, who followed him in expectation of some grave disaster. The lodge was only a short distance from where they were. It was an untenanted little cabin that had at one time been used as a shooting-box on the Crabbenden demesne.

All-three entered together. The single room of which it was composed was dark as pitch—the light, through window, chink, or fire, being carefully excluded.

So strange a circumstance instantly awaked O'Hara's suspicions. He plucked Colthurst by the coat, and whispered, "Come away!"

They turned. The door was slammed to behind them, and everything was dark as the grave.

"'T is a trap!" shouted O'Hara, with all his force. He felt for his pistols. He had them in his hand. He rushed for the door—had his hand on the latch—when a blow from some heavy weapon descended on his head, and sent him senseless and bleeding to the floor.

The same instant Colthurst's herculean frame was pinioned—heavy hands pressed him down on his knees, while thick cords were gathered round his arms and breast, and tightened till they almost suffocated him.

"Villain!" he thundered, half choking with rage and pain, and apostrophizing Crofts, "this is your work. Ruffians, release me!"

He could utter no more, for big, brawny hands were forcing a gag into his mouth. The giant at length was helpless.

Then the door was thrown open, and the morning light streamed in on this savage scene. On the ground lay the senseless form of O'Hara; Colthurst, securely bound and bursting with agony of mind and body, still writhed helplessly in the grasp of his captors; three villainous-looking scoundrels, armed with heavy bludgeons; Captain Crofts, designer and artist of the entire tableau, stood contemplating his work with imperturbable coolness.

"Bless my soul!" he cried, gazing round in affected astonishment, "have we fallen on a den of murderers? How, villains?" he added, turning to his myrmidons— "what is the meaning of your assault on this gentleman?"

"Captain Colthurst is arrested under the king's writ," said one of the fellows, flourishing his warrant, "for £97 6s. 2d., due to John Markham, Esquire, Clonmel, and I warn all loyal subjects not to interfere with us. We are the officers of the law."

"Oh! indeed," cried Crofts, with undisturbed serenity. "I'm sorry for you, Colthurst—especially sorry because we can't finish that little duel. Lord Crabshawe will be tearing mad for being baulked of his game—but we must all respect the law, old fellow. 'Tis the fortune of war —that's all—and you have only to make the best of it."

Colthurst replied to him with a glance of withering scorn, and motioned to his captors to lead on.

When O'Hara recovered from his stupor, he found himself stretched, numbed and suffering, on the sward outside the lodge. As the cause of his unconsciousness gradually came to his mind, he leaped up, and discovered that, except a chill through his frame, and a painful soreness on the head, he had sustained no injuries from the adventure.

He hastened to the lodge and found it deserted. Colthurst was gone—he knew not where! He could not even guess the motive of the base ambuscade that had been laid for them. Still less could he account for his being himself left unharmed. He could scarcely believe that Lord Crabshawe would be a party to so base a device; yet no other explanation was at hand. What story could he give Lucy of her brother's disappearance? How should he ever face her with so dire intelligence? Then the episode of the bailiffs the previous night occurred to him, and afforded him some clue to the mystery.

He recollected that the dog-cart which brought them was fastened at the foot of the hill. On the impulse of the moment he jumped into it, fled, rather than drove, into Clonmel, and ascertained that his friend had been conveyed into the debtor's prison there an hour or two before. Satisfied in some degree with the scant intelligence thus gleaned, he returned towards Kilfinane Cottage to break the news to Miss Colthurst.

When he reached the cottage, Lucy was sitting in modest morning attire, at the open parlor window, gazing out on the clear frosty sky, with those bright orbs that seemed to pierce the blue vault, and hold converse with her kindred shapes above.

Hesitating to disturb her placid dreams, O'Hara had gained the middle of the room, sad and dubious, before she turned round and saw him.

As she did so, she almost screamed, and a flush of crimson mantled her cheek, when she perceived, with woman's quick eye, the blood oozing through his matted hair, and the generally tossed aspects of his habiliments.

"Be calm, Miss Colthurst, I entreat you," cried O'Hara, as he sprang to her side, and supported her with his strong arm.

"My brother—Oh! Mr. O'Hara—my brother!" she cried.

"Believe me, there is no cause for alarm," said O'Hara, earnestly.

"Oh! tell me, Mr. O'Hara—in mercy, tell me!" and she looked up to him with those pleading eyes in which her anxiety had lit an irresistible fire.

"I assure you solemnly he is safe!" cried O'Hara, half intoxicated with that magic glance.

"Thank God!" she exclaimed. "But what—what has happened him?"

In a few words he repeated their adventure of the morning, making it appear, however, that Colthurst's arrest was effected in the ordinary way.

She listened to him in rapt attention, her heavenly face beaming with an unspeakable wealth of love, and varying with her emotions like a summer sky.

"My poor Jack," she cried, a flood of tears at length coming to her relief. "Man must indeed be powerless where you've failed. Yet, perhaps, it were better so. There, at least, he will be safe." Then suddenly starting up, "I will go to see him, Mr. O'Hara," she cried resolutely.

"Alas! there is no use thinking of it," said O'Hara.

"How! Surely they will let *me* see him?"

"Yes, but you see there are forms to be gone through. I tried to see him myself, and they told me visitors were only allowed in on Tuesdays and Saturdays."

"And can nothing be done for him before Saturday?" she asked, half imploringly

"Yes, Miss Colthurst, very much. I will myself see that he is well treated while he has to remain there. But it appears some Dublin official or other must come down to estimate the assets, before anything can be done for his release."

"Alas! what then can *I* do!"

"Make your mind perfectly at rest, I implore you, Miss Colthurst. At the earliest moment possible he shall be free. I have myself a purse of three hundred sovereigns, the thoughtful gift of my dear sister, and that shall speedily purchase his release."

"Oh! you are too generous, Mr. O'Hara," she cried, with a sweet smile through her tears.

"Would that I could prove it more effectively!" sighed O'Hara. "But stay!—how about the election?"

"Alas! I suppose there is an end of it. Poor Jack had set his heart on that election."

"Heaven! I see it all now!" exclaimed O'Hara, a sudden thought striking him. "The villains! They removed him because they were afraid of him. Well, well, they shall be baulked."

"They shall?"

"They shall, if man can do it. Should it go to the worst, I will myself take his place on the hustings, and force their base treachery down the ruffians' throats."

"Oh! would you also expose yourself to needless danger?" she asked, half appealingly, and alarmed at his angry looks.

"Nay, my dear Miss Colthurst," he replied with a smile, "it shall be only a matter of words, not blows. Besides," he added, in a softer tone, "I cannot forget that poor Jack has committed *you* to my guardianship."

"Me!" she exclaimed, with a perceptible blush.

"Yes, you, dear Miss Colthurst," he said fervently. "You are not pained at the trust?"

"Oh! no, Mr. O'Hara," she cried, extending her hand to him with generous, confiding freedom, while her soft eyes beamed with unutterable gratitude. "I already owe you more thanks than a lifetime could repay."

He kissed the little hand so lovingly placed in his.

"You shall best repay me, my dearest Miss Colthurst," said he passionately, "by not speaking of the trifling things I *have* done. Rather give me the opportunity of doing more for your sake, and I shall indeed be happy."

"Thanks, thanks!" cried the fair girl, her cheeks suffused with blushing pleasure. "Believe me I shall know how to rely on your friendship."

"Nay, on my love—my love, dear Lucy!" cried the young enthusiast, in a transport of affection, sinking to his knees and clasping her unresisting hand.

She was pale and red by turns, but not with anger—it was love—a trustful, all-confiding love, that brooked no concealment. It was heaven's own pure fire that glowed on her cheeks, and lighted up her beautiful eye.

She did not withdraw her hand from his; but the memory of her recent grief subdued her rising emotions.

"Do not—do not speak of love now, Mr. O'Hara," she cried, averting her eyes; "this is no time for such a subject."

"True, true, dearest Lucy," assented her enraptured lover; "I am too selfish, while poor Jack is suffering. But happier times will come, do not fear. Dare I *then* hope that you will look more favorably on a heart's first love?"

And between two young hearts, burning to commingle their deepest affections, what should have been the answer but one?

CHAPTER XIII.

THE OUTLAWS.

THE course of our story brings us back to Glengarra. Later in the day on which Captain Colthurst was captured, Milly O'Hara sat meditating gloomily in her little boudoir. A wonderful change had come over her since we last met her—a change all the more marked because of its abruptness. She, who had never seen beyond the silver lining of life's cloud, was now enveloped in the sad shades of their sable reverse. The loss of a brother whom she adored, the blight of a home in which she had been happy—these were griefs weighty enough for a novice in sorrow. But her heart spoke of one other dolor, more subtle, but more potent than the rest. Why disguise it where it could not be denied? It was the loss of a lover.

Whether she loved (in the extravagant sense of that term) Jack Colthurst, she had never decided, and even yet doubted; but that their sudden separation had drowned all other sorrows in its overwhelming grief, it was hopeless for her to deny. No feeling of hers had ever before been prisoned—she now felt her whole heart and soul set on Jack Colthurst. Like a thunder-shower over an embrowned plain, her chastening crowd of sorrows had forced into blooming life the thousand flowers of womanly affection that were but sowing in the early springtime of her glad innocence. Thoughts that she had scarcely dreamt of, flitting through her young fancy, shaped themselves into dawning facts, and with the bitterness of grief came its sweet consolations.

But, alas! what a change those twenty-four hours had worked. The smiles were gone; the laughing word, the satirical *nonchalance*, the unreflective spirit—all faded; on her brow, the settled image of grief—on her features, the play of new and graver passions. Yet the change was not a disagreeable one. On the contrary, her wild beauty sat more resolute and more grand in the tearful garb of woe.

Sitting there, white and rigid as a statue, her eloquent eyes shaded by their long lashes, and her clustering black hair gleaming like an ebon setting, she looked more truly the woman of man's noblest dream than in the most joyous days of her light-hearted life.

Presently a light tap at the door aroused her from her meditation.

"Come in!" she said, sadly, scarcely moving her head.

The door opened and in stepped Lord Crabshawe, rigged out in the pink of the fashion, and, to all appearance, at perfect peace with himself and the world.

"Lord Crabshawe!" exclaimed Miss O'Hara, rising to her feet, and glancing rather angrily at the intruder.

"Yawz, my deaw Miss O'Hara," commenced his lordship, advancing timidly, and helping himself to a seat near his companion, "I must beg youaw pawdon for—for alawming you "——

"You needn't speak of it, my lord," said Milly, coldly; "*you* haven't alarmed me."

"Why, bless my soul!" cried Lord Crabshawe, surveying her with childish awkwardness, "you look vewy pale, and all that, don't you?"

"I can't say," said she, curtly; "I haven't examined

myself. I could not have foreseen your lordship's visit."

" Aw!" pursued his lordship, pausing in the vain effort to disentangle his ideas. "Yawz, but you don't look the thing, you know—you used knock a fellaw about so—you were so jolly. Pawdon me, deaw Miss O'Hawa, has anything annoyed you?"

"Oh! nothing that would interest you—many thanks for the inquiry," said Miss O'Hara, in the same haughty tone. "But can I do anything for your lordship?"

The question was so abrupt that it nearly made his nervous lordship jump. He blushed like a girl, then muttered a *sotto voce* malediction on his stupidity, and then took to twitching his hat in helpless imbecility. He probably meant to make a declaration of love, as Milly could easily augur from his timid side-glances at herself, and his evident distress at not being able to master some pretty compliment.

At length the absurdity of his position nerved him to a desperate energy, and, sinking to his knees, he seized hold of Miss O'Hara's hand, shouting in a theatrical voice:

"Do you love me?"

In happier times Milly would have laughed outright at his grotesque attitude and the comic sincerity of his face. As it was, she withdrew her hand calmly, and without moving a muscle, replied:

"Your question surprises me, my lord. You surely cannot expect an answer."

"Think, deawest," he continued, plucking a little audacity now that he was committed to his position. "I love you—as the bwightest staw in the fiwmament of—of —— I adowe you. You awe the only woman I could love. Be mine, deawest. You shall be happy as the biwds of pawadise."

This high-flown verbiage he had culled out of some tale of Spanish chivalry, and delivered with all the ridiculous magnificence of Don Quixote de la Mancha. In spite of her grief Milly could scarcely refrain a smile as she answered:

"Oh! impossible, my lord. Pray don't say any more on the subject."

The rebuff brought Lord Crabshawe to his senses, and discovered him as the laughable fool he was in his attitude of sublime gallantry. The reaction brought a fit of equally stupid anger, and, like a bold child, he whined out:

"I can see thwough it. If 'twas Captain Colthuwst that asked you, you wouldn't be so weady with youaw fwowns."

"Lord Crabshawe!" cried Miss O'Hara, bending on him a look of withering anger and contempt.

"I knew it," cried his lordship. "Pewhaps, then, you'd like to know that youaw favowite is this moment in Clonmel gaol."

"In Clonmel gaol!" echoed Milly, completely crushed by this fresh blow.

"Yes; in Clonmel gaol," repeated Lord Crabshawe, with spiteful emphasis. "Moawe than that, he wefused to fight a duel with me this moawning, and he has given up his absurd pwetensions foaw the wepwesentation of the county, and"——

"Stop!" cried Miss O'Hara, recovering her proud composure, and glancing fiercely at the creature at her feet. "It's a lie, a base invention. How and when has Captain Colthurst been captured?"

"Last evening, by two bailiffs, at his own house," said Lord Crabshawe, who to do him justice was ignorant of the real means by which Crofts had managed the capture.

Milly felt her heart almost breaking with pain.

"Ha! now have I moved you?" cried his lordship, again seizing her hand. "Be mine, and you awe foaw eveh happy."

She drew herself up with a stern majesty that awed her suitor, and pointed to the door.

"Lord Crabshawe," she said, firmly, "leave the room this instant, or I shall have you whipped out of it like a dog."

Awed, astounded, and almost senseless, Lord Crabshawe raised himself half mechanically from his kneeling posture, and shrinking from the magic power of those eyes, slunk from the room, overwhelmed with confusion.

Scarcely had the door closed on him, when the pent-up feelings of her woman's nature at length gave way in a flood of tears. Then, dashing the glittering drops from her cheek, the brave girl rose resolutely to her feet, and, with the energy of her strong soul, cried out:

"Yes—he shall be saved! No more grief now; there's work to do."

No sooner was the resolution formed in her mind than it took effect. The last tear-drop was brushed from her cheek, a new fire was kindled in her eye, and a fresh energy braced her drooping spirits. She summoned her faithful old nurse, and, to that lady's extreme surprise, ordered her to procure one of those heavy cloth cloaks, with ample hoods, commonly worn by the peasant-women of the time. Her orders were obeyed, for Nanny loved her darling with a warmth that made her humor her every wish.

"Now you may retire, and return to me when it gets dark. I am going to Slieve-na-mon to-night."

"To-night, Miss Milly!" exclaimed the nurse, in utter amaze.

"Yes, yes, Nanny, to-night," she rejoined, impatiently. "Don't be teasing me now, Nanny. I am resolved."

Nanny had never seen her child so grave and so terrible-looking before; but she did not dare to break in on her impatient mood again.

As soon as the early day had closed, and the darkness descended, Milly O'Hara and her nurse might be seen hurrying along the snowy road from Glengarra, wrapped up closely in their heavy mantles. The night was dark and windy, fitful showers of sleet adding to the discomforts of the exterior world. The two women hastened on bravely through the pitiless gloom, and, after a long and weary walk, began to ascend to higher and more mountainous ground, where the rough path was encumbered by uneven masses of stone and ruddy channeled intercourses.

Shortly the path altogether disappeared, and misshapen piles of rocks shut in the vision on all sides. From the raw thinness of the air, it was evident they had reached a considerable height on the mountain. But still higher they ascended—through untracked ways, along savage gapes of rock—buffeted by the sleet, affrighted by the lonely shrieks of the wind through the hills, encompassed by perils, drenched, torn, and benumbed; yet buoyed up by that invincible solace—a woman's purpose.

In the thickest of those fastnesses, sheltered by million-shaped rocks, safe in its utter isolation, was a rude shieling or hut, propped up with mud and wattles in a gaping crevice of the mountains. It was towards this wild habitation, the nominal home of a gruesome old hag, that Milly O'Hara now sped on her mysterious mission.

She knocked with a peculiar tap at the door, and receiving no answer, repeated the summons.

This time a rough voice from inside sang out—
"Who's there?"

"ONE OF THEM!" replied Miss O'Hara, firmly.

"Why, surely, that should be an angel's vhice," cried the same person, dubiously. "Howsimiver, angel or divel, you can't do us much harm wid a vhice like that."

The rude door was unhinged—a brawny form, with blackened face and gleaming blunderbus, stood in the passage.

Unflinchingly the brave girl advanced and raised her hood.

"Miss Milly!" cried the man, falling back astounded, and bowing reverently to his visitor. "Surely, 'tis yer ghost I see here at this hour o' the night."

"No, Andy, no; it is myself," said Miss O'Hara, hurriedly. "Can I see the Captain?"

"*Machree gal*," cried the huge fellow, his eye dancing with honest affection—"'tis I that's enthranced at the sight o' you. Yerra, my darlin' child, what's the matther wid you? Why, you're kilt intirely wid cowld and wet."

"Oh! thank you, Andy," she replied, touched at the fellow's simple admiration. "There's nothing wrong with us! Tell me, can I see the Captain?"

"Yerra, to be sure you can, me jewel. Come on wid me. They're all in the council inside, an' 'tis glad the Captain will be to get a look at yer purty face this night."

He led her across the dark passage, and, having exchanged a further countersign, another door was pushed aside, and gave entrance to a rough-hewn cave. This second chamber was weirdly illumined by an oil-lamp, whose yellow glare fell on fourteen or fifteen men grouped in eager conclave around an improvised table. The time, the place, the weapons glittering in the light, and the fierce aspect of the men themselves were meet accompaniments of a tribunal at whose terrible fiat the brand and the bullet capped the dread *vehmgericht*.

At the new arrival, the men leaped to their feet simultaneously; then, recognizing their visitor, an astonished and delighted murmur ran round.

"Miss O'Hara! Welcome, Miss Milly!"

And then delight broke into a cheer as the fair girl advanced into their midst, and cordially returned their greeting. Well might they have been profuse in their welcome, for many a time and oft had Miss O'Hara, the proud lady of Glengarra, sheltered their band from the pursuing hand of justice, and won them by her entreaties from the very jaws of death.

She now advanced to the head of the table, where, vested with the rude semblances of authority, sat one whom we have met before—the dark-visaged Joe Hogan, the outlaw chief.

As she approached, his sullen face lit up with a mingled reverence and affection, and those features, furrowed with harshness, and imprinted with crime, warmed into a smile as he bid her welcome.

"Captain," said Miss O'Hara, "I have come to ask you to do me a favor."

"Name it for me, miss—name it," he cried, eagerly, "an' if 'twas to swim through oceans o' blood, the Rovers are at your sarvice."

A chorus of eager assent broke from the assembled outlaws.

"Thanks, thanks, men. I knew I might count on you," cried Miss O'Hara, warmly.

"Ay, to the death for Glengarra! Name your wishes."

"Captain Colthurst has been taken——"

"And what of that?" demanded the Captain, the sullen scowl returning at the mention of the name.

"I want you to rescue him!"

"Rescue *him!* Impossible!" thundered the outlaw, with an oath, all his savage enmity aroused.

"Impossible!" echoed Miss O'Hara, growing pale with despair.

"Ay, *impossible!* He insulted me vilely, yesterday—yes, *me*—the Captain of the Rovers—he spurned and disarmed me, and I've sworn that I'll have revenge."

"But for *me*, Captain," cried the fair girl, her heart almost sinking within her—"for me!"

The outlaws shouted with approbation; but the black scowl rested on the Captain's face.

"Not even for you, Miss Milly," he said, determinedly. "I will die for you, but don't ask me to give up my revenge."

"Oh! have a nobler revenge," cried the lovely creature in a tone of agony. "Take revenge by saving him. I kneel to you, Captain," she cried, dropping on her knee in an attitude of entreaty. "For *my* sake, will you grant it?"

"Heaven itself couldn't stand agin you," exclaimed the hardy outlaw, at length, flinging off every vestige of sullenness; "for once, and for your sake, I forgive. Rise, Miss O'Hara, I didn't mean you to kneel to me. One word from you would bend the world."

"Thanks, oh! a thousand thanks," she cried, as she rose, beaming with satisfaction. "Now I know he is safe."

"Ay, safe as if he was here this minnit," cried the Captain, warmly. "I would lose my life for him now, for your sake."

The outlaws chimed in a gleeful assent.

"Whin was he taken?"

"This morning."

"He's in Clonmel gaol, I suppose, now!"

"He is—the debtor's side."

"All right. 'Tis out o' the question to do anything to-night. To-morrow he'll be free, if I'm a livin' man."

"The nomination takes place at ten—could he be then free?"

"He'll be there in time, believe me."

CHAPTER XIV.

AN IRISH ELECTION.

On the morning following the events related in the two previous chapters, Clonmel, the county town of Tipperary, presented a singular spectacle. It was the day for the nomination of candidates for the county, and such days were devoutly set apart for the most extravagant excesses. The present election was, however, different from the generality of its fellows, in the fact that the people were in earnest. Other elections were periods in which the lower classes, distrustful of all candidates, embraced that side where most money, drink, and excitement were to be had for their howling. On this occasion it was their own champion that was in the field, and they felt they had something tangible to fight for.

The fame of the contest, disseminated and enlarged upon by the secret organizations, had penetrated the whole south riding; and, at early morning, thousands set out for Clonmel, from every town and hamlet, to give their voices and their arms to the popular candidate.

Long processions of stalworth men, marching under the ensigns of a new liberty, blocked up the roads, and affrighted the morning by their furious enthusiasm. None dared to resist the popular tide; all followed, exulting and unreflecting, under the influence of that intoxicating excitement that follows the enfranchisement of the slave. To do them justice, it must be added that their infant freedom was as yet unstained by excess: for once they were determined in their purpose, and faultless in their demeanor. They felt that they were daring everything in the cause, and the nobility born of the sacrifice lifted them above disgrace and dishonor.

Sweeping into the confined streets of the town, those tributary streams of humanity swelled into one vast, seething ocean of men, who completely overflowed the narrow streets.

But soon through those vast masses went words which stilled their enthusiasm and staggered their purpose. The news of Captain Colthurst's arrest reached them now for the first time. With it came a vague rumor, originated, of course, by the minions of Lord Crabshawe, that his arrest had not been unpleasing to himself. In fact, with the exaggerations of malice and distrust, it was soon openly bruited about, that Captain Colthurst had connived at his arrest as a cover under which to sell the brave hearts that had been pledged to him. Everything gave color to this heartless calumny. His arrest as a debtor (illogical proof of his liability to money temptations)—his neglect to make arrangements—the downcast looks of his known confidants—every circumstance whispered treason; and to a confiding people, the very suspicion of betrayal poisons reflection.

As these rumors multiplied, the aspect of the crowd underwent a visible change. The blind enthusiasm of the morning vanished under the foul breath of suspicion. The natural reaction set in — a sullen, suspenseful gloom. Their unity—the one guiding object—fell to pieces, with its supporting enthusiasm. The crowd broke up into groups; shame and resentment spoke from every face; they were no longer powerful—only a vengeful disorganized mob.

The countless spies in the service of Lord Crabshawe

were not slow in reporting these encouraging symptoms, nor were his agents less tardy in fomenting them, and turning them to advantage. They despatched among the crowd a number of trusty employees who circulated the most crafty and circumstantial accounts of Captain Colthurst's treachery: how the story of his arrest was a fabrication; how he had got a purse full of guineas and had gone off to the continent; and how—crowning device of ingenuity—he had furnished Lord Crabshawe with a black list of those who were pledged to vote for him, in order that the landlords might be able to visit them with summary punishment. To strengthen the effect of the story, public houses were thrown open, in which drink was dispensed freely to the mob—money was scattered broadcast among the poorer classes—and threats and promises were urged with double eargerness. Then, when the popular mind was sufficiently prepared, a squad of drunken rowdies was got together, who paraded the streets, decked out in the national fashion, bellowing in unsteady accents, "Owld Ireland for ever," and, "Down wud the thraitor."

From time to time silent-looking men might be noticed gliding through the crowd, and then disappearing with a few of the more determined. But anything like open opposition was terrified into silence, as a gaily caparisoned troop of dragoons, with flashing helmets and jingling swords, galloped haughtily through the divided crowds, on their way to the court-house.

Thither now poured the stream of human beings. At that period election time was considered a warrant for unchecked license; and the court was entirely abandoned to the mob, who filled galleries, seats and dock in a closely-packed mass.

The bench was improvised as a hustings, and here, to the right of the sheriff, stood Lord Crabshawe and his immediate friends. All of them looked delightfully at their ease. This miscellaneous group of noblemen, landlords and attorneys, now satisfied that they had an open field, condescended even to hold gracious converse with the mob, several of the most uproarious and dangerous of whom they nodded to in the most fascinating way. Lord Crabshawe himself, though unable quite to master the situation, was in the blandest humor, agreed with everyone and on everything, and said deliciously stupid things to people he never met before. All of which was swallowed most cheerfully by the mob.

On the side of the hustings set apart for the friends of the opposing candidate stood, with folded arms and gloomy brow, Charles O'Hara. He was the sole representative of the opposition, and even he himself was doubtful whether he came there in opposition.

His position was indeed an uninviting one. Colthurst's arrest had devolved on him an amount of responsibility to which he found himself unequal. On the one hand, he knew that his friend had set his heart on this election, and that nothing would give him more pain than to lose it by so untoward an accident. O'Hara's own convictions, too, told him that now or never, while the popular enthusiasm was aroused, could the people's battle be fought, and he could easily foresee how irretrievable a blow would be struck at the national movement, if the present opportunity were lost. But, on the other hand, he felt himself almost powerless to carry on the contest. Colthurst was himself the only repository of his own schemes. O'Hara was quite ignorant of the extent of his pledges, his system of agency, or, in fact, any single arrangement for carrying out his designs.

Fortunately, he knew a few farmers in the neighborhood, who, in compliment to himself, consented, after much pressure, to come and nominate Captain Colthurst in his absence. But this was the only arrangement he found it possible to make; and now he found his position more untenable still, when he looked round in vain for any token of sympathy with the absent candidate—when, on the contrary, the rumors of Colthurst's treachery, and the maledictions poured upon him, came to his ear from every part of the court-house. His farmer friends even resolutely refused to expose themselves to the vengeance of their landlords and of the mob, by nominating a man whom everyone pronounced a traitor.

This desperate position of affairs, though it crushed out every hope of success, only steeled O'Hara to a higher resolve. The odious calumnies heaped upon his friend, he found himself bound by a thousand claims to dissipate and hurl in the face of their dastardly author. The election itself, he gave up as a bad job, but he was determined that at least the triumph of the enemy should not be complete. One friend alone stood by him in that gloomy hour—it was Mick Hoolohan, whose spirits even were depressed by the attitude of affairs.

The business of the election commenced with the reading of the writ, during which Lord Crabshawe's friends preserved a self-satisfied smile. Then the sheriff expressed his readiness to hear anyone who had a candidate to propose.

Sir Emanuel Cavendish, a haughty baronet, who had crushed more serfs than any two in the county, stepped forward to propose Lord Crabshawe, and was cheered as if he had been a demi-god by the grovelling cowards who would have murdered him if they dared. The proud baronet felt and showed his contempt of their slavish homage. Without one acknowledgment of the ovation of the mob, he turned to the sheriff and pronounced the brief formalities embodying the nomination of Lord Crabshawe.

His seconder was of a different stamp. Ebur Grundle, J. P., was a nervous, irritable little man, who feared the sight of an armed peasant as he would an earthquake, and who was accordingly reduced to the necessity of conciliating a shadow of popularity among a people whom he detested. He was somewhat of a *novus homo*, who had earned his place and his title in an English rag-and-bone shop, and was patronized by the aristocracy because he was a useful tool between themselves and the peasantry. Mr. Grundle seconded Lord Crabshawe's nomination in a smilingly stupid oration, in which he talked of the benefits that would accrue to old Ireland, and "her noble and generous people," by the return of a man like his candidate, "who loved his country, and desired to see her elevated to her proper place beside the great British nation." He then spoke with an eloquence slightly *fade* of the ridiculous pretensions of a foreign adventurer who came here to sow the seeds of discord and unhappiness between landlord and tenant, and to sever that holy union of interests which should always unite them in such gatherings as he had the happiness of seeing round him to-day. This nameless revolutionist had had the prudence (or the dishonesty—Mr. Grundle feelingly added) of abandoning his criminal enterprise at the last moment; he had betrayed the wretched dupes whom his promises might have led astray; but he (Mr. Grundle) was only sorry that he had not had the courage to show himself on this hustings, until he would see how grossly he had mistaken the spirit of the gallant people of Tipperary, if he imagined they would desert their country and their best protectors for a nameless and penniless stranger.

And again the unreasoning plaudits of the mob broke

forth in acknowledgment of this condescending oration, and the few that listened with shame held a prudent silence, while Mr. Grundle withdrew, satisfied that he had stored up for himself a weight of popularity that would save him from stray bullets for many a day to come.

Then, when silence again fell on the assemblage, the sheriff stood up in conscious dignity, and asked, smilingly, had any other elector a candidate to propose.

O'Hara glanced round with blazing eye and burning heart for his friends. They were nowhere to be seen. A chorus of "No, no!" greeted the sheriff's question from the rabble. Lord Crabshawe and his friends smiled superciliously, and glanced with satisfaction at the crowd.

"Has any other elector a candidate to propose?"

A moment's suspense! Again no answer but the jeering shouts of the mob and the smiles of the victors. All, then, was over—nearly all!

"Has any other elector a candidate to propose?"

"Yes!" thundered O'Hara, as he leaped to the front of the hustings.

Lord Crabshawe's friends looked from one to the other. O'Hara was assuredly one of themselves—he was not certainly going to betray them; yet anxiety was already preying upon their unruffled prospects.

A silence deep and solemn brooded over the scene. Every eye was strained to the speaker.

"Hear me!" he cried, his full voice rolling sonorously through the breathless silence; "you've been asked is there any other candidate to propose. *Is* there any other candidate to propose? Your hearts tell you there is—your mouths fear to speak. Is there a *man* here? —one man among the thousands that dared to be more than slaves! Have you souls? Have you *anything* that is not thralled and emasculated by slavery? You are men to all outward seeming—you have the power, you have the nerve, you have the forms of freemen—will you not have their hearts? The choice is before you! You may liberate yourselves now—the time, the power, the man, has come. Or—and mark you well the alternative—you may reject the chance, once and forever, and remain sunk, as you have been, in the abyss of degradation, a shame to the world, and a torture to yourselves. It is enough, Irishmen—your silence makes answer—you choose the fortunes of the coward slave."

Under his burning invective, the shrinking mob crouched like whipped hounds—the eyes of their masters were fast riveted upon them—eviction and ruin still paid the penalty of freedom. The landlords, amazed and awed by the fiery eloquence of the young tribune, still hesitated and feared.

One alone had the fortitude to break the calm.

Captain Crofts shouldered jauntily to the front, and assuming an aspect of the deepest concern, cried out to his shrinking myrmidons:

"Well, you hear yourselves called slaves, men. Will you not prove that you're no cowards?"

"Ay, he calls us cowards!" shouted a few of the most brutal of the mob; "down with him!" and five or six of the most villainous of the scoundrels flourished their bludgeons threateningly in his face.

But the more honest and determined were now in their turn aroused. Ringing cheers for the speaker broke from all parts of the court-house, and numbers of stalworth, determined men, pressed eagerly after his aggressors.

O'Hara was unmoved. Crofts' wanton interference intensified his fervor. Again his voice rang clear and loud over the angry tumult.

"I was wrong, fellow-countrymen. There *are* men among you still; but there are also fiends in human shape. I care not whether any among you be bold enough to nominate Captain Colthurst—he cares not himself—he entered on this contest not to fight his own battle, but the people's—ay! to raise you—you, who now execrate without hearing him—from a degradation and misery worse than death. If you dread to follow his lead, be it so—yours is the loss if you rivet your own chains faster. But one thing you *must* know—silence! men, till you hear it—'twill bring confusion to knaves—'twill gladden honest men—Captain Colthurst has been *betrayed!*"

"Betrayed!" broke from the breathless masses, in an ominous eagerness.

"Yes! basely, treacherously betrayed—betrayed by the very men that come here to win your voices. I am, myself, the witness. My Lord Crabshawe, whom you are called on to elect, challenged your candidate to fight, and played on his courage to entrap the man whom he was afraid to face honestly. Captain Crofts, the gentleman now so solicitous about your character for bravery, was the base tool of this infernal plot."

"A lie, a d——d lie," vociferated Lord Crabshawe stunned and trembling.

"Mr. Sheriff," cried Crofts, with a superhuman effort to retain his calmness, "I call on you to stop this young man. He is no elector, and has no right to speak here."

"Villain!" cried O'Hara, boiling with passion, "I have the right of an honest man."

"You shall answer, sir, for this. Mr. Sheriff, I appeal to you."

But appeal was now heedless as to an ocean. The hot words of O'Hara worked a miraculous change in the posture of the mob. They saw at a glance that they had been befooled and betrayed, and in the first impulse of passion, they rushed in an angry column towards the hustings.

Suddenly, outside the court-house, a thunderous roar of cheering was heard. It swelled louder and louder, till it drowned the commotion within. The tramp, as of a mighty multitude, came nearer and nearer. The court was hushed in expectancy. A rush—a confused roar—a mighty influx of men—and the court-house shook with the thunders of acclamation that rose from every man.

O'Hara glanced wildly, confusedly, at the new throng. In their midst, hoisted on heads and shoulders, a giant frame towered up above the rest. He came nearer and nearer—bowing, laughing, huzzaing—another thunder of cheers and Captain Colthurst himself leaped on the hustings, and grasped his friend's hand in an embrace of iron!

"In God's name, Jack"——

"Hush! man alive—it's glorious."

The gallant captain stood proud and happy, facing the countless masses that had by this time flooded the court, and made it ring again with their deafening acclamations. His honest face glowed with triumph; but it glowed also with sterner feelings.

"Hear me, men," he cried, at length succeeding in stilling the applause; "I am here, to-day, for a double purpose—I come to avenge you, and myself. Both of us have been basely betrayed."

The multitude thundered an angry assent. Their resentment now in full swing, execrations on Lord Crabshawe and his principal supporters became loud and general. A tumultuous rush of men rose to the platform, and, armed with fierce hearts and strong bludgeons, swarmed on to the hustings.

But the objects of their enmity had beaten a hasty retreat. Where Lord Crabshawe and his friends were a few moments before victorious and supreme, not one of them now awaited the storm of popular fury they saw approaching. Through the rear of the court-house they fled in the direst dismay, and every agent of theirs slunk away in terror, or joined the popular current.

So instantaneous was the change, that O'Hara, a moment since battling against a crowd of enemies, could scarcely realize that he was now the centre of an innumerable host of friends. But so it was: the victory of the people was resistless, unexpected and complete!

Disappointed that their timidity had foiled his secret revenge, Colthurst was yet amazed and delighted at the sudden change affairs had taken.

"Enough, men, now—enough," he cried, in vain endeavoring to make himself heard in the deafening roar of voices; "our enemies have fled—let's to business."

Powerless himself to restore order among that swaying mass, he beckoned to one of the most prominent of the mob, a tall, dark-visaged man, the author and agent of this wonderful scene. The man turned and disclosed the well-marked features of the outlaw "Captain."

"I kep' my word, captain," cried the outlaw, with an expression of delight that seldom crossed his scarred features; "I've brought you in time, an' no mistake."

"You did, Joe, you did," said Colthurst; "I can never forget it. But now let's not lose the opportunity. Clear off your men, and let us finish the business."

The leader of the Rovers sounded a long silvery peal on a whistle, and as if by magic silence was restored. The signal of the Rovers passed through the dense throng, and like lightning the invading host retreated in quiet to their places.

The poor sheriff had witnessed those strange scenes in wonderment and dismay. Himself an intimate friend of Lord Crabshawe, and a decided lover of aristocratic institutions, he would gladly have postponed the election or left the court but for the resistless attitude of the mob. He well knew it would be death to cross their wishes now, when they were supreme and determined. So, though in his heart bursting with rage, he conformed outwardly to the spirit of the hour, and made a desperate effort to seem impartial.

"I have asked twice," said he, in a tremulous halting tone, "whether any elector has another candidate to propose. I ask now for the last time."

Ere he had finished speaking, an actual crowd leaped on the table and proposed Captain Colthurst.

Another thunder of applause shook the building, and the sheriff's further questions went unheeded.

The poor little man once more thought of resistance —but he was a drop in the ocean—the thousand fierce faces blazing around him were argument enough.

"I will now call for a show of hands," he said, with the air of a man who was suffering slow martyrdom. "All who are in favor of Lord Crabshawe will please hold up their hands."

A howl of execration and of coarse laughter was his answer. Not a hand was held up!

"Those who are in favor of Captain Colthurst will please hold up their hands."

A forest of hands started up from end to end of the court-house. There could be little dispute as to who had the majority.

"I hereby declare the show of hands in favor of 'Captain Colthurst," said the sheriff, nervously.

The applause again broke forth in a deafening storm. No one knew what was to come next.

O'Hara stepped forward:

"Mr. Sheriff," he said calmly, "no poll is demanded on behalf of Lord Crabshawe. He has evidently withdrawn from the contest. I therefore call on you to declare that Captain Colthurst is duly elected."

The sheriff was in tortures—he would have given much to be within hail of the troop of dragoons; but there was no safe alternative but submission now: afterwards the whole thing could be annulled.

"Does anyone ask for a poll on behalf of Lord Crabshawe?" he asked.

Not a voice was raised for the powerful nobleman, who only yesterday might have ruled them with a rod of iron.

"There being no opposition," resumed the sheriff, "I hereby declare Captain John Colthurst elected "——

"Duly elected," suggested Colthurst with a significant smile.

"Duly elected to represent Tipperary in parliament."

Again and again the roar of voices thundered over the scene, and a people long strangers to anything but serfdom, rioted in the excess of their new-born reedom.

The new member—the people's choice—gazed proudly on that sea of upturned faces, and listened with delight to the music of their rejoicings.

"I'm *your* member, now," he said, at last. "This is no time for making speeches, even if I was able to make one. You know me well, and all I can say is, if you don't like me—you now have the power—kick me out as you have kicked me in. You've done everything. I've done nothing. But I tell you what I *will* do—I'll take right good care that Crabshawe, Crofts, and Co., shift their rascally wares to some other market from Tipperary. One word more. You are freemen—prove yourselves worthy of being so. Now, boys, three ringing cheers for Ireland, Tipperary and—our excellent friend, the sheriff."

And the poor gentleman was ovated by the rabble, until he began to fancy himself a rebel of the first water.

CHAPTER XV

EN SUITE.

CAPTAIN Colthurst was member for Tipperary—elected swiftly, and without a struggle—but he knew too well that the sudden and violent proceedings by which he had been "pitchforked into office" were not likely to remain unpunished. Lord Crabshawe and his powerful supporters had fled under the influence of panic; but that panic must be shortlived; and, with authority and military force on their side, they might attempt to overthrow the popular triumph. Besides, he could not forget that he had been himself rescued with violence from the hands of the law, and that he and his chief supporters stood at the present moment in the light of outlaws. These reflections suggested a plan, which he carried out with the imperturbable coolness of the perfect soldier.

Being well acquainted with the shaky timber of which the sheriff was made, Colthurst determined on making use of him as a shield for himself and his friends.

"Your arm, Mr. Sheriff," he said, gripping the functionary's arm with an exquisitely courteous but suggestive hug. "I'll pilot you to the door."

"Oh! many thanks: but you know"—

"But what?" demanded Colthurst, resolutely.

"Oh! nothing; only I wouldn't like to—to"——

"Don't mention it, my dear fellow; we quite understand each other;" and he carried off his unwilling, but unresisting captive.

The vast crowd began to surge in confused masses towards the doors, and Colthurst escorted the sheriff, followed by O'Hara, and a few of his more intimate friends, into the thick of the crush.

When they reached the doors, Colthurst had reason to felicitate himself on his foresight. Right in front of the entrance was drawn up the troop of dragoons, with their swords drawn, ready for the charge, and at their head the redoubtable Captain Crofts, who, in his capacity of magistrate, had assumed their command. Crofts' evil-looking face was pale with passion, and his eyes scanned the out-coming crowd with eagle glance.

Immediately that he saw Colthurst his face blazed with vindictive light.

"Arrest that man! Charge, soldiers," he cried wildly, pointing to the new member, and setting spurs to his horse.

Colthurst replied with a calm sneer.

"Let 'em come, captain," whispered the outlaw chief from behind. "One signal from me an' every throoper there will be a dead man before he is ten minutes older. Say the word, an' I'll sound the whistle."

"No, Joe," replied Colthurst; "no bloodshed while we can do without it. Mr. Sheriff," he added, turning calmly to the trembling creature on his arm, "we're under your protection here. Tell that officer I'm a particular friend of yours."

"Oh! nonsense, sir!"

"Don't delay, please."

"But it's im-im-p-ossible."

"Speak, sir, *immediately*. The Rover Captain is at your ear."

"But they're going to charge."

"Order them not. Cry out halt!"

"H-h-ha-lt!" shrieked the terrified sheriff, and the officer of dragoons repeated the command.

"This gentleman is under my protection," suggested Colthurst.

"Th-this g-gentle-man's under my pro-tection," gulped the sheriff, shaking like an aspen leaf with rage and fear.

"Stand back there, soldiers, stand back; I'm under the sheriff's protection," repeated Colthurst, with an easy smile.

"Confusion! he's an outlaw—a gaol-breaker—a murderer," shouted Crofts, utterly beside himself with rage at this unexpected turn. "Charge! I order you. I'm a magistrate."

"Tell him you're sheriff, and as such have command of the military," whispered Colthurst to his trembling victim.

"I—I—eh—eh—I"——

"Sdeath, man, out with it. Pause, and you're a dead man."

"Yes, yes!" faltered the unfortunate sheriff; "I'm in command here. Officer, I forbid you to stir."

"Oh! this is outrageous," cried Crofts, foaming with passion. "I tell you he's an outlaw. Order, or no order, I tell you arrest that man. You dare not disobey me."

"We are under the sheriff's orders alone," said the officer of dragoons, haughtily.

"Enough, sir, let me pass there," said Colthurst, determinedly. "As for you, Captain Crofts, keep silence, or I shall have you taken into custody for disobeying the orders of the sheriff."

With inimitable coolness Colthurst and his friends cleared their way through the crowd. On the street, close by, stood a handsome light carriage which had conveyed Lord Crabshawe to the courthouse. Without an instant's deliberation, Colthurst piloted his friends to where the carriage lay, still dragging the unfortunate sheriff with him as a guarantee of safety.

He leaped into the carriage, and seized the reins. O'Hara and Hogan had just time to follow him.

"Good-bye, Mr. Sheriff. Many thanks for your protection. Crofts, we'll meet again. Good-bye, friends all. Hurrah for Tipperary and its gallant sons!"

A thunderous shout of applause went up from the mighty multitude. Touched with the silk, the highbred horses started off rapidly. The crowds gave way—another roar of voices cheered them—the open street was reached, and the fugitives were safe from their astounded pursuers.

Ere they turned the corner, another mighty roar of voices broke forth—shrieks and shouts mingling in the din. The dragoons were charging—their bright blades flashing in the sun; but a wall of living men had closed around them, a thousand shillelaghs were raised, stones came pattering in a deadly shower—a long and desperate struggle wrapped the combatants in a cloud of tumult. Ere it ceased, Colthurst and his daring companions had fled past the town, and pursuit was hopelessly checked.

Their horses were in splendid trim, and the miles were covered at a flying pace. Sensible that they were now safe, for the time being, at all events, the young men gave themselves up to the rejoicings natural on their success.

"It *was* a splendid piece of strategy," said Colthurst complacently.

"Splendid is no name for it. 'Twas superb."

"And Crofts the infernal villain!"

"I'll settle that gintleman," said the Captain of the

Rovers, with an evil scowl; "I've a private account with *him*."

"Not before me," said Colthurst.

"And why not, pray?" asked Hogan, with that air of insolent authority he usually wore.

"Simply because I forbid you, man."

"Forbid me!"

"Come, come, don't let's quarrel again, Joe; you know you're bound to be a friend of mine, now."

"Well, well, let it be so. I *am* bound captain. If I wasn't, I wouldn't submit to be dictated to."

"Pshaw! It's foolish to talk that way. You know I wouldn't annoy you. I owe you my freedom."

"You needn't thank me for that," said the other, sullenly.

"By Jove! I had quite forgotten that, Jack," said O'Hara. "How in the world did you get released?"

"That's more than I can tell you. All I know is that I was walked out of prison by my friend, the Captain, here."

"Yes; 'twas done swift and sure enough, wasn't it?" said Hogan, with a grin of satisfaction. "But niver mind! 'Tis a sthrong gaol the Rovers couldn't turn inside out."

"But how did you do it?"

"Oh! that's a saycrat. We've a friend *inside*. Where haven't we, I'd like to know?"

"Well; but what did he do?"

"Just got fifty good min inside the walls, allowed us to knock down the couple o' warders, an' open the door of your crib."

"By Jove! 'twas deliciously daring! I fancy to-day's business will make the king tremble for fear we might take it into our heads to run off with himself. But your motive is the strangest part of the thing."

"Ay! indeed, captain; I give you my word you'd

keep the inside of the goal if I had my wish. I don't mind tellin' you honestly I'd be your inemy till death only for some one that takes an intherest in you."

" And you won't satisfy me as to who that person is?"

" I'm bound not—but I tell you agin you may thank her an' not me for bein' free this minnit."

" Her! Then it's a woman."

" Tare-an-agers, man, aren't you satisfied yet?"

" You're right, Joe; I won't trouble you with any more questions on the point, though I would like dearly to know who my guardian angel is. However, give her my best respects, and tell her if at any time she cares to see her *protege*, I'll give her a *cead mille failthe* at Kilfinane."

" And as I live," cried O'Hara, " while we've been talking we've reached Kilfinane itself."

There it was—the cosy little rose-trellised cottage; and there at the door was its born goddess. The glad tidings of her brother's rescue had reached her by some channel, and at the sound of the wheels she rushed, beaming with smiles and happiness, to the door, in time to clasp her beloved brother to her breast, as he descended gaily from the carriage.

O'Hara thought she had never looked more beautiful than now, in her dazzling white costume, her sunny hair floating in volumes round her marble neck, and the joyous fire of happiness stealing softly through the sad brilliance of her eyes.

" Why, Lucy, you must have thought me fairly lost by this time," said Colthurst, as they entered the cottage together.

" Oh! Jack, I was very unhappy about you," she murmured, leaning her head trustfully against his heart; " I had such horrid dreams, that I think I'll have to give up all faith in dreaming—'tis so happily deceitful."

"Yet, you don't *seem* very unhappy, dear," said her brother, patting her flushed cheeks fondly. "I fancy I've had a very worthy substitute in my friend Charlie."

Lucy blushed scarlet, and O'Hara's cheeks took a heightened color. The young lovers glanced timidly at one another, as if ashamed of the concealment, and anxious that it should be ended; but an electric consent told both that it would be premature.

Colthurst noted the mute episode, certainly without pain.

"Well," said he, frankly, "I knew I was putting the right man in the right place, when I left Charlie my executor."

"Only that I've had but a very brief term of trust," said O'Hara, with a smile.

"You may thank Joe it hasn't been longer," said Colthurst turning to the outlaw, who had remained a silent spectator of the scene.

"What! was it you, then, sir, that released my brother?" cried Lucy, turning to the dark-featured Rover, with eyes eloquent with gratitude. "Then, indeed, I am your debtor, for I owe you the very light and motive of my life."

"Yer eyes 'ud repay the debt wid intherest, Miss," said the Rover gallantly.

"Take care you don't transfer too much of your allegiance from your mysterious lady," put in O'Hara, laughingly.

"P'raps a trifle o' yer own allaygiance is due to the same lady," said the outlaw, with a curious smile.

O'Hara started—the thought struck him for the first time—did not Milly take an interest in Captain Colthurst? More vaguely and diffidently the same thought occurred to Colthurst. Perhaps if the reflections of both of them had been laid bare, the possibilities of the future might become the facts of the present. But fate never weaves life's textures without knots and cross-stitches. Their fancies were dismissed as chimerical.

Lucy, to whom Hogan's allusion was a riddle, busied herself in providing for the creature comforts of the men. This duty over, she had the whole story of the rescue and the subsequent scenes at the court-house rehearsed to her, and listened with that deep thankfulness and shuddering dread of past dangers which are the surest indications of an affectionate heart.

Then came the all-important subject—their plans for the future.

The outlaw soon relieved them of suspense on his account, by announcing his determination to return to Thurles immediately. He was not yet tired of his life of perilous adventure, and had still many a feud to avenge among the great ones of Tipperary. That night the Rovers had to burn down Lord Montiford's farmyard, the next they were to settle scores with a bailiff at Carrick.

"We'll meet again soon," cried Hogan, as he drove away in Lord Crabshawe's vehicle.

"I sincerely hope we won't," said Colthurst, as he returned into the parlor. "Now there goes one of the most consummate villains in the land."

"One of a class of cut-throat bravos that gives me a thorough distaste for an Irish revolution," said O'Hara.

"Yes—the fellow has a brute ambition to climb to notoriety on a pedestal of slaughtered corpses. Fortunately he is illiterate, or he might be another Marat. But his class are necessary. In revolution the greater villain is the better soldier; society rights itself after a time."

While they were talking a horse galloped up the path at a furious pace, and checking him suddenly as he came to the door, Mick Hoolohan leaped breathlessly from the saddle.

"Run, run for yer lives!" he shouted, as he burst into the room, puffing and blowing like a porpoise, "the sogers will be here in a jiffey."

"What! where have you come from?"

"From Clonmel, to be shure."

"Well, and what's going on there?"

"Such slaughter I never seen! The whole place is in a ruction. The sogers are bay'netin' an' killin' like divils, an' stones are flyin' as thick as plover. Oh! be the powers, they'll be down on ye if ye don't make haste, an', indeed, I wudn't care to come to close quarthers wid 'em in their present humor."

Lucy was pale as marble, but wonderfully collected. The young men looked at one another gravely.

"'Tis true," said Colthurst, at length. "Those soldiers are very savage when they're aroused. I fear our election triumph will be shortlived."

"By no means," said O'Hara, firmly. "'Twas worth the sacrifice. Nothing will wipe out the disgrace of the landlords but our punishment, and there I think we can easily baulk them."

"But there's no time to be lost."

"Time enough, however, for calm deliberation. If what Mick says be true, the handful of dragoons will be hard enough occupied for some time without abandoning the town to come on a wild-goose chase after us."

"By Jove! you're right, Charlie. But what's to be done? I propose to arm ten or twelve of the natives, and give the fellows a hot reception if they come."

O'Hara smiled at the rash proposal.

"No, Jack," said he "we must abandon the fortress. God knows, enough life has been lost already, without shedding more blood uselessly."

"Right again, my boy. It would be useless. But how could we abandon the place?"

"That's the question," said O'Hara, with an anxious

look; "if we fled ourselves, we should leave Miss Colthurst here, and that I'll never do."

"I have it, Jack," cried Lucy, suddenly starting from her reverie, and displaying a singular amount of resolution in her unflinching glance. "You recollect my dear uncle in France?"

"The very man, Lucy," cried Colthurst, "you are becoming a general as well as an angel. But you forget—we haven't heard from him for a full year, and he was in the thick of the campaign in Vendee—perhaps he's dead and buried six months ago."

"But I have his address in Paris, and his family are surely living: you know how often and how eagerly he pressed us to join him."

"Lucy, you're a perfect jewel! we'll off to Paris then—but confound those obstacles! how to get there is another question."

A sudden and happy thought flashed across O'Hara's mind. He remembered the packet given him by Frank Inkston that night in the chambers at Trinity College, containing introductions to the members of the French Directory, and instructions how to proceed in Dublin so as to obtain fuller directions and secure a passage to France. Here was at once an occupation suited to his adventurous tastes, an escape from the perils around them, and a certainty of securing the companionship of the being now so closely knit into his affections!

"Hurrah!" he cried, joyously—"a brave thought, by Jupiter!"

"Let's have it, Charlie, by all means," said Jack.

"You've no objection to joining me in an embassy from the United Irishmen to the French Directory?"

"On the contrary—rejoiced! But *qu'est-ce qu'il vaut?*"

"Simply that it frees us from a very awkward predicament. Here, then, is our plan. You and I set out for Dublin to-night—we're quite safe there for a couple of days. I have introductions to the Council. They are desirous of sending an embassy to hurry the armed intervention of France, and will be very glad to get two like ourselves, without ties or fears. A nod from them will procure us a passage across, and once over, we will have had a second triumph over the Tipperary potentates. As to Miss Colthurst, we cannot ask her to share our flight to-night; but she can stay for this night with some friend, and can easily rejoin us in Dublin, when we've made all our arrangements for the voyage."

"Oh! admirable! You are a tower of sense, Charlie. Who would have thought it from your roguish blue eyes?" cried Colthurst, joyfully.

"Oh! it's exquisite!" exclaimed Lucy, glowing with excitement and delight. "And to see dear, lovely France again! O Mr. O'Hara, you've quite changed me. I'm almost glad of this day's adventures—they promise so soon to rid me of this life of anxieties and perils."

"Then indeed I am happy," cried O'Hara, fervently. "But in more peaceful times we may have feelings—at present we cannot afford to indulge them. How about Miss Colthurst for this night?"

"Oh! easily settled," said Lucy herself, "I'll go over and stay with Father Ryan to-night. There they will not dare to follow me."

"Then our last care is smoothed away," said O'Hara. "Mick will haul out the fly in no time. Then a short adieu to dear old Tipperary, and 'Paris ho!' is our cry."

CHAPTER XVI.

LORD CRABSHAWE IN DEFEAT.

On the evening of his precipitate flight from the hustings at Clonmel, Lord Crabshawe and Captain Crofts sat over their wine in the dining-room at Crabbenden. His lordship's face seemed like the playground of emotions, too infantile and shapeless to make their presence more ruffling. There were anger, and rage, and disappointment, and disgust, and numerous other little mental maladies disporting themselves over his countenance, twinkling in his eyes, twitching his nose, and pulling his brows, and playing hide-and-seek among lips, teeth, and moustache. So distraught was he by the variety and incongruity of those little shapes of passion, that he could scarce make up his mind whether to stamp the world under foot, and smash to pieces the naughty thing; or to administer defeat a haughty hand-and-foot, and sit down with dignity under the shadow of his disappointment; or whether, after all—and this was a thought of Crabshawe, Crabshawish—there was anything to be particularly annoyed at. Such piecemeal reflections he transferred from his overworked brain into his glass of Madeira, and strove hard to pound them into some intelligible resolution in the rich clear liquid, which, somehow, seemed to him much fitter for the drudgery of thinking than his own unsteady cranium. Yet, still all the little emotions seemed to be dancing round the wine, and playing with the thought, until the noisy hum lulled his lordship into that delicious state of irresolution where he dreamed that the best thing he could do was nothing.

Not so Captain Crofts. For once that placid gentleman was in a towering passion. Not that he was very red, or very blazing to outward seeming. Captain Crofts always *used* his passions: he seldom let them use him. But the rebellious sprites were peeping out in spite of him through the sparkles in his eye; they were climbing industriously over his smiles, and striving for mastery with all the funny things he said. And they succeeded so well, that the word "baffled" was stamped plainly on his forehead in the hieroglyphs of rage.

The dinner was over without allusion to what had passed. The two men—or rather, the nobleman and gentleman—loitered over the wine in the hope that its rosy key would unfasten the dead-lock into which they had shifted. Crofts was drinking the red current; Crabshawe was diving in it listlessly, seeking the vague thought that seemed buried in its bosom.

At last the captain broke cover, though not in the old slap-dash style.

"Egad, it is good, isn't it?" he said, meditatively.

"Yawz!—best bin in the cellaw," said his lordship, still hankering drowsily after the thoughts that he knew were swimming about somewhere in the wine.

Again a pause—a communion with the soft grape—and Crofts cantered out cautiously from his retreat.

"I tell your lordship what," said he—this time forcing a big, unwieldy smile down the throat of the struggling passions—"we should lose no time in repairing this day's work: it's one satisfaction that we'll have revenge swift and sudden."

Lord Crabshawe said "Yawz," because it was a respectable reply, exacting no great waste of energy; but he was still deep in the Madeira, searching, searching for the bright idea buried in its crystal cells.

"There's one thing sure," pursued the captain, "we have them on the hip about the election—it wouldn't hold for a moment. It's a monster joke, the whole thing;" and the captain chuckled convulsively.

"Yawz," assented his lordship, holding up his glass eagerly against the light, and still diving thoughtfully into its depths.

Crofts was disconcerted. He could not understand his patron's coolness, or the unmeaning blank that covered his face.

"Confusion, my lord!" he cried half testily, half jocosely, thumping the table with his fist, "is this my affair or yours? One of our fellows would have fought ten duels for half the provocation. Don't you know that you've been insulted—driven out of the representation of your own county? Not only you, but all of us—all of us! By gad, my lord, our order has been disgraced by this rebel varlet!"

The passions were the victors over the captain, and they sat grinning and howling in triumph in every line of his face.

"Aw," remarked Lord Crabshawe, yet deep in his search for the vinous inspiration, "aw, wight, Cwofts, wight;—but—I—I don't hawf know—that is—what's to be done?"

"Done!" cried the captain, half contemptuously—"why, leavé for Dublin this very night—have this infernal mockery of an election annulled at once—then set the government on this rascal, Colthurst: and if you don't care to kill him yourself"—this with a broad and palpable sneer—"let somebody else kill him that's able."

His lordship laid down the glass, as if he had found what he wanted. Without heeding in the slightest what his friend had just said, he drawled out slowly and deliberately:

"Well, Cwofts, to say twuth, I hawdly know—at least, I'm hawf inclined to think—confound it, I mean to say—aw—that—in fact—that, dem it! it serves us wight."

"Serves us right, my lord! Surely you're joking. Why, the fellow hasn't left us a shred of honor."

"Aw—but you see—aw—it seems to me—hang it! I cannot well say—but I don't believe we've left much of that to ourselves."

Crofts was dumbfounded. Such sensible remarks from his lordship set him utterly at his wit's ends.

"I can't understand your lordship!" cried he. "Men don't usually talk so when a fellow has insulted them. You cannot forget that Colthurst is M. P. for Tipperary."

"Yawz, twue!"

"That you have had to fly for your life from the rascal's presence."

"Yawz."

"And, besides, that he has baulked *me*. Ay, and the man who baulks Ben Crofts had better look out—that's all."

Lord Crabshawe glanced once more at the Madeira, as if to gather new resolution, and then proceeded calmly:

"Well, Cwofts, my ideaw is that—that Colthurst is a fine, bwave fellaw. You know we didn't—ahem—act very fairly towards him. He has beaten us, and—and I'm hawf inclined to say I'm glad of it. I'm sick of this soawt of thing. I—I like fine, honest men, and, hang it, I like Colthurst; but I like Chawlie O'Hawa bettaw still. Fact is, Cwofts, they've beaten us decently, and —and—they hawf deserve it. Besides—aw—to tell twuth—aw—Milly O'Hawa likes Colthurst, and—and she doesn't like me; and—and—in shawt, my deaw fellaw, I'll leave the best man win—that's all!"

After delivering himself of which disconnected burst of eloquence, his lordship smiled benignantly, with the air of a man who knows he has said a good thing and awaits the admiration of the world. If he expected Crofts', he reckoned without his host. That gentleman's face was dyed purple and green with rage; and his voice trickled harshly as he rejoined: "Can I trust my ears? Let the best man win! What, under heaven, does your lordship mean to do?"

His lordship enjoyed his astute friend's confusion immensely. He looked, positively, a sage, as he replied calmly:

"I shawn't do anything."

"What! Let this madcap's election pass unchallenged?"

"Certainly."

"And let a red-hot rebel represent Tipperary!"

"Even so—he's a genuine fine fellaw."

"And put the finishing touch to his triumph and our disgrace."

"Yawz—let the best man win."

"By all the gods, you're mad, my lord," cried Crofts in uncontrolled rage.

"No, Cwofts, I was always a fool, I think, till this moment. I'm in earnest now."

"But you would be for ever disgraced—you could never show your face again in Tipperary."

"I don't want to," said his lordship, coolly. I don't care for the people, and they don't care for me. I'll go back to England to-morrow—somehow I get on bettaw there."

"The devil you will," cried Crofts, gruffly. "It matters little where a coward like you goes."

Lord Crabshawe took in impressions by slow draughts, and it was some moments before he fully mastered the extent and deliberation of the insult. Strange to say, he betrayed no very lively emotion—late events had quite accustomed him to the belief that his dignity was not above mortal reach, and now, in the freshness of his new faith, he was by no means ready to take any further rebuffs amiss. He was a little pink in the face, but scarcely otherwise disconcerted, while he replied:

"If I be a coward, you are a villain. I don't hawf know which is the moaw cweditable."

Crofts glared at him like a tiger; he seemed anxious to strangle him on the instant, but he forebore.

"Perhaps, after all, my lord," he said, in a conciliatory tone, "'t were better for both of us not to quarrel."

It was now his lordship's turn to take the offensive.

"Well, Cwofts, I think 't were bettaw we did. Fact is, Cwofts, I hawf like fine honest men, and you—aw—you're *not* an honest man."

"Then you would get rid of me?"

"Well, yaws, I think so."

"Idiot!" shouted Crofts, in an unbridled fit of passion. "Were you worth shooting, you should pay for this."

The self-possession of the young nobleman was wonderful.

"This time," he said, "you shall find me a match for you."

He walked deliberately to the bell-pull and touched the bell. In a moment the call was answered by a footman.

"Show Captain Cwofts to the doaw," said his lordship, with a stiff bow to his companion.

Trembling with baffled rage, Crofts saw himself for once outwitted; but there was no help for it. He had only to bow as best he could, and retreat in undisguised confusion.

When he was gone, Lord Crabshawe threw himself in his easy chair, and laughed until he nearly cried. It was his first exchange from the listless command of a puppet to the proud victory of a man, and he liked the transfer immensely. He never before knew what it was to enjoy doing good; for now he knew well that he had done good.

He tossed off the sparkling glass from which he had drawn his inspiration; and he smacked his lips most contentedly, as if he knew he had swallowed an oracle of good sense.

Then the footman was summoned again, and Lord Crabshawe forthwith penned a note to the high sheriff, declaring his satisfaction with the result of the election, and his desire that Captain Colthurst's victory should be ratified. Then, while the fever of beneficence was upon him, he despatched another note to Milly O'Hara, telling her he was leaving the country next day, asking her pardon for his cruel stupidity, confessing that he had been an ass, and promising to be a good boy towards everybody. Then he gave orders in hot haste to have everything ready for his immediate departure for England.

And then he leaned back once more in his chair, and sipped his Madeira, and thought—oh! how glowingly—what a much better figure he cut in his new character.

CHAPTER XVII.

DUBLIN IN THE OLDEN TIME.

EARLY on the evening succeeding the election day the carriage containing Charles O'Hara and Jack Colthurst entered the confines of Dublin. Mick Hoolohan had left them a few stages back, on the excuse of providing quarters for them in the city; and, jaded by the length of their journey, the young men were dozing away the time drowsily, when sounds, as of a distant clamor, struck their ears.

It was already quite dark. They were passing through the thick thoroughfares of the Liberties, where the fetid rows of gaunt houses and the heavy yellow fog shut in the view on all sides. For a time only an indistinct clamor reached their ears. Then, suddenly, a short turn of the street set them full in front of a vast multitude winding along the narrow thoroughfare. The shifting lights of blazing tar-barrels and pine-wood torches, lustred the long lines of faces, and pictured the scene in flaming hues. The hoarse blare of trumpets and the heavy beat of drums, timed with the trampling of the crowds and the occasional roar of voices, gave it the appearance of some great popular pageant.

Presently the carriage of our friends reached the front of the procession. A horseman dashed out of the crowds with a flaming brand, and held it to the carriage window. then turned with a wild cry, and shouted to the people at the top of his voice, "Hurroo! boys, here they are!"

By the torchlight, O'Hara recognize the face of Mick Hoolohan.

Even as he spoke, a mighty sound swelled through the heated street—cheers—yells of enthusiasm—rolling of drums—a wild tumult of sounds.

"Tipperary for ever!" "Erin-go-bragh!" "Hurrah for our member!" and such like watchwords, shouted in their immediate vicinity, solved to the friends the secret of this extraordinary display. Hoolohan had proceded them in order to spread the news of the great popular triumph, and to organize this unlooked-for ovation for the young heroes of Tipperary.

Remonstrance was useless—words were as orders to the ocean. In a twinkling the horses were unyoked—the postillions and their team engulfed in the crowds, and the carriage whirled along by a hundred willing hands.

Young, ardent, and impulsive, both the friends felt no difficulty in accommodating themselves to the popular temper, though, at a calmer moment, both might be tempted to question its prudence. As for Mick, he careered so proudly on his charger, and exerted his lungs with such effect, that, in the uncertain light, many began to mistake him for the M. P. for Tipperary.

Through a wilderness of tall dingy streets they passed in procession, and, momentarily increased in numbers, struggled on to the greater thoroughfares.

Here the national enthusiasm had communicated itself to the wealthy burgesses. In the rich warehouses and lofty mansions there were windows blazing with illuminations, and crowded with fair women, who poured down their favors on the popular pageant as it moved past. From every street and lane came accessions to the throng—now rude bands braying—anon green banners waved in the torchlight—and ever over the tumult came the hum of multitudious voices, and the tramp of innumerable feet.

Presently, as they passed up Dame street, and emerged into College-green, the vast multitudes broke into one instinctive shout of frantic triumph, as the carriage was born through the yielding crowds on to the very steps of the Parliament House.

It was a great debate night in the Irish Parliament—one of those sure presages of what was to come, that so often preceded the Union. The vast square was the very image of a nation's forum. Its stately piles of architecture—its blaze of lights flashing from gilded balconies—the pomp and splendor of its surroundings—but, above all, the wide sea of faces swarming over the square, and flowing far into the side streets, and down to the river, proclaimed that there indeed was the heart whose vigorous pulses forced the life-blood of prosperity to the uttermost extremities of Ireland.

The arena in front of the House of Parliament was crowded with gay equipages and gorgeous liveries. Peers and commoners mingled in the brilliant throng; beautiful women, whose breasts and foreheads sparkled with costly gems, were alighting from their carriages; men whose eloquence had pealed through the world conversing in the porticoes; all was life, animation, and magnificence—the radiance reflected from healthy national existence.

With throbbing hearts our friends' eyes wandered over the brilliant scene, and proudly they reflected that their own struggle for fatherland was one of its moving springs. Colthurst's big heart was especially carried away, and over and over he grasped O'Hara's hand joyously, pointing to the countless masses, and whispering: "Heaven! isn't that a people worth saving?"

Almost as their carriage was drawn towards the

steps, a flourish of trumpets from the direction of the Castle announced the approach of the viceregal *cortege*. In eloquent silence the wide multitudes separated to let it pass, and the princely show—the prancing of steeds and the clattering of swords and flashing of bright uniforms—went by unnoticed; the while the plain equipage freighted with the Tipperary M. P. engrossed the eyes and voices of thousands.

But now came reflection—for they were already within the precincts of the Parliament House. They had never intended to go near the House at all; for both were agreed that the proceedings at Clonmel would not be long allowed to stand, and they naturally supposed, too, that the escape from the gaol and the flight of Lord Crabshawe's friends would give ground for an inconvenient investigation, ending, doubtless, in their arrest and detention.

Little they suspected that at that very moment a messenger was arriving, bearing the sheriff's full ratification of the election.

A hurried consultation decided their course of action. Alighting from the carriage, they were instantly hoisted on men's shoulders, amid the frantic applause of the populace. His youth and fair face attracted the most considerable attention to O'Hara, who leaped nimbly from his human cushions on to the top of the carriage, where he was immediately joined by Colthurst.

"Speak to them first, Charlie," whispered the captain. "I'm half nervous."

O'Hara doffed his hat, and waved his handkerchief smilingly. The light of the torches made him visible to the entire multitude, whose deafening applause rang again in his ears. Then a breathless silence. His clear, ringing voice sounded far into the stillness, as with all the energy of youth he exhibited its headstrong precipitancy.

"Irishmen," he said, "I thank you, not for myself, but for the nation. While Ireland has yet hearts like yours, her future beams with promise. Here, to-night, standing on the threshold of an assembly where your liberties are being corroded, and your independence undermined—here in the first flush of the victory Tipperary has won for you—here, let us make a new pact with our representatives. My gallant friend, the member for Tipperary, shall set the seal to it. He wishes, men of Ireland, to address you, not your rulers—to appeal, not to the Irish parliament, but to the Irish people—to abjure, in short, a worthless government and a corrupt chamber, in whose fatal atmosphere our country's liberty lies dying. Henceforth let the battle of Ireland be fought *outside* the House of Commons—the People's will be the Parliament of the future!"

Like wildfire the young man's hot words ran through the masses, who rocked and swayed in their transports of enthusiasm.

And then, when silence again hushed the scene, Colthurst spoke.

"Countrymen," he shouted, at the top of his kindly voice, "I don't take this night's demonstration to myself. But I take your hands for Ireland's sake, and I say her heart beats true as ever. Irishmen, I never was much of a set speaker; but I'm a soldier, and all I can say is, I think the sooner you're all soldiers the better. *Then* I'll be able to talk to you, and no mistake. My friend here has told you more than I could say. As he says, I henceforward turn my back on the House of Commons. Meanwhile, boys, let's have three cheers for old Ireland, and three more to our next merry meeting."

"And three more for Tipperary!" yelled Mike Hoolohan, as the mad cheers tore through the sky, and drowned all else in their great volume of sound.

In the wild confusion that followed, O'Hara and his friend disappeared dexterously in the throng, and soon lost themselves in the ever swelling tide of humanity.

Through the din and the tumult they shortly found themselves drifting in the eddies of the crowd towards Grafton street. Just as they finally emerged from the hot press into the cold air, another tremendous cheer broke from all sides of the square at once, and with its echoes came to the young men the news that somebody had announced the sheriff's confirmation of the Tipperary election.

O'Hara strained his eyes over the swaying multitude, and recognized the earnest face of Hussey Burgh proclaiming the intelligence to the excited populace.

They little guessed at the time the meaning of this puzzling news. Nor did the majority on the Treasury benches, to whom the news came as a scathing brain-blow.

But, even did he know the truth, there was now an impassable gulf between Captain Colthurst and the constitution. Both he and O'Hara had voluntarily cut themselves adrift from it, and were being swept along with all the overmastering force of the tide of revolution.

The next evening Charles O'Hara was closeted with the chiefs of the United Irish organization, and received from them, for himself and Captain Colthurst, the missio to the French Directory.

Despatch was, above all things, pressed upon him, but he needed small stimulus to hasten as far as possible his departure from the country.

He received ample directions how to proceed. The smuggler, in which he was to take passage, would sail from Wexford in a few days; and he received every suggestion that could aid him in escaping detection while still in the country.

Lucy Colthurst joined them the following day; and the three bid good-bye to Dublin with light hearts. Youth's eager fancy was already painting the clouds that hung over their lives with the silver hues of hope. But oh! how fate will daub those pretty pictures with his rough, black brush.

CHAPTER XVIII.

IN THE MOONLIGHT.

THREE days after, a light bark was standing out from a little haven on the Wexford coast, and speeding away over the waves.

In the moonlight, two figures were moving on deck. While Jack Colthurst was being initiated in the mysteries of the smuggling craft by the fire in the forecastle, Lucy and O'Hara were out under the stars, dreaming and thinking, and gazing pensively back at the blue line of coast retreating behind the horizon.

It was, for the season, a beautifully clear night. The stars were in the heavens in glistening groups. Streams of soft moonlight were pouring along the distant coast-line, and went roaming dreamily over the wide waves, like an army of silver battalions, now pitching their snowy tents in the hollows of the sea, now spread in glittering review over the swelling billows.

The air was solemnly hushed. The blinking of the timid stars, the soft whisper of the wind, and the subdued rustle of the water around the keel, seemed only as the mystic communion of airy spirits. Angels might have been astir in the bright, clear atmosphere.

The two watchers sat gazing in rapt silence. Their hearts were too full for utterance—full of thoughts of life and love—full, too, of the dreamy fancies of the hour, which tinged the darkness of their present with the radiance of trustful hearts.

Far from feeling as fugitives, chased by a thousand

cares, and embarking on a perilous future, whose end they knew not; they were living in a bright little world of their own, all crystal with hope and love, where care carried not his wrinkled front, and life was crowned with flowers. What heaven must be, when earth can own such bliss!

Farther and farther retired the misty shore, and they watched it as, time after time, it sank into the blue. It was hardly more than a speck, when the moon rose suddenly over its heights, and crowned it, as it were, with a pearly diadem. Then it faded in distance, and there was no longer anything but sky and water.

The change startled the dreamers simultaneously.

"Poor Ireland!" exclaimed Miss Colthurst, sadly, still gazing where it had disappeared.

"Are you also, then, so grieved to leave it?" asked O'Hara.

"Grieved! oh! yes—I had learned to love Ireland passionately."

"Yet, Lucy, you have not been very happy there."

A faint blush reddened her cheek. She answered with downcast eyes.

"Oh! yes, I have been happy. Jack's wild ways often made me uneasy, and—and—perhaps I have been sometimes lonely. Somehow, I could not like the rude, heartless society of Tipperary."

"Who could, unless a barbarian?" interrupted O'Hara.

"But for the people themselves, I shall never forget their kindly hearts: to see them happy has often, often been the delight of my lonely hours."

"Bless you, dearest!" murmured O'Hara; "to see you must, indeed, have been happiness to them. It is seldom a ray of sunshine crosses their path."

She blushed at the ardent compliment, but smiled sweetly.

"Don't make me chide you for telling fibs, Charlie," she said. "But see! The last glimpse of land is gone. Oh! how lovely is it now in the Galtees! How often I've watched the white moonbeams straying over the meadows, and playing on the blue mountains. How softly the little brook must be tinkling down in the valley. And dear Kilfinane!—ah! how I'd love to see it once again!"

"With all its misery and wretchedness?"

"Mercy! how you spoil the picture! But even so—one may love things for their very misery."

"But France—beautiful France, that you are going to?"

The fair head drooped, and a tear glistened on the long eye-lashes.

"Yes, I love France, too," she said, sadly; "but it is for the memories of my life there." She paused abruptly, and her tears came fast.

"Many pardons, dearest Lucy," cried O'Hara, eagerly. "I did not mean to pain you. You know I did not."

"Yes, Charlie, I know you did not," she said, smiling through her tears. "The memory of grief comes softly to me now. I can even bear to revisit the scenes where I suffered so much when a girl."

"And could you even bear to revisit the scenes of your happiness in Ireland?"

"Bear! It is one of my fondest hopes."

"Then you shall, dearest Lucy," cried the young man, enthusiastically. "You shall return to an Ireland happier and freer than the Ireland you have left—you shall return to it when we have cleared it of its misery."

She sighed softly.

"Doubt it not, dearest Lucy," he cried, in the same

earnest strain. "Heaven must prosper us. And if it does, Lucy—if we can return once again to a free and happy land, dare I hope"——

The aspiration was rudely cut short by the apparition of Colthurst on deck.

"How, young people!" he cried, gaily. "Studying astronomy, eh? I shouldn't wonder a bit, Lucy, if the deceiver was after telling you that there's more astronomy to be learned in your face than in the whole milky way."

Lucy blushed and smiled.

No, Jack," she cried, "but we've been bidding good-night to dear old Ireland."

"Well, well," said Colthurst, buoyantly, as he scanned the far horizon, "I hope we'll be bidding it a happier good-morning one of those days."

And thus they said farewell to Ireland.

CHAPTER XIX.

'TWIXT LIFE AND DEATH.

It was a bright clear day in the early spring, when our travellers caught sight of the sun-tipped minarets and domes of Paris.

Being unencumbered with luggage, they travelled in an open *caleche*, just large enough to accommodate them, and give Mick Hoolonan a seat on the box.

The sky was of that heavenly blue that Paris skies alone can boast, just freshened by a brilliant sun. As they emerged from the dark *closeries* of the Faubourg St. Antoine, into the gay thoroughfares of central Paris, they found plenty of food for abstracted reflection and delight in all they saw around them. For Colthurst, everything suggested some old pleasant association, and opened out to him anew the scenes where he had reaped honor and pleasure; for Lucy, it was the renewal of the tender days of girlhood, when a mother's love yet shielded her from the world; for O'Hara, it was one long panorama of fresh wonders, the nursery of that mighty revolution whose heavings pierced the world, the palace of a gorgeous romance.

Here the republican soldier could point to where he had followed the *sans culottes* in the bloody days of September—where he had fought with Westermann, and shouted with Danton—where Louis had died, and Mirabeau had spoken. There, Lucy could trace where the guillotine had stood—where the shrieks of a mad populace had sounded her father's *requiem*—where a broken hearted mother knelt beneath the cold, bleak scaffold. Young and enthusiastic, O'Hara could only see the City of the Revolution—the dauntless people that had stormed the Bastile—the glorious fanatics who had overthrown the legions of tyranny.

Each engaged in such meditations, they passed rapidly through the populous avenues running parallel with the river.

As they entered the Rue St. Honore, signs of some great public rejoicing began to present themselves. The street was spanned in various places by triumphal arches, laden with flowers, and inscribed with mottoes of republican triumph. Tricolor flags hung out of some of the windows, and others floated from the roofs of the houses. The shops were decorated with flowers and evergreens. On the sideways and at the street corners bands of women and children began to collect, some bearing republican ensigns, all having joy and enthusiasm depicted on their countenances. Among them mingled the old fierce type of the *sans culotte*, men with hollowed cheeks and glazed eyes, attired with an affectation of recklessness, and looking as though they were again forming for the charge on the Tuilleries.

Presently, and before our friends had well entered the street, the sound of martial music was heard in the opposite direction. Immediately, with a shout of "Here he comes!" the scattered bands flocked in the direction of the sound. At the same time, the close streets opening on the Boulevard gave forth their squalid population, and the Rue St. Honore was covered with a motley crowd.

In a few moments the head of a military column made its appearance—then bands and banners—and then a long line of cavalry, infantry, and artillery. The bands were playing the fierce refrain of *ca ira*, which was echoed as fiercely by the bronzed veterans, and shouted from the thousand throats of the spectators.

The carriage of our travellers drew aside to let the procession pass. O'Hara watched the splendid pageant as it moved onward, with fascinated gaze. The soldiers were all of them bronzed and war-worn—the remains of the magnificent citizen army that was after hurling back combined Europe from Alsace. The uniforms of many were dust-covered and imperfect; but the enthusiasm that lighted up their scarred faces recalled vividly the death-defying fanatics whom Pichegrue had led to victory.

Anon the tumult became more deafening, and the enthusiasm more uncontrollable, as the uniforms of the staff-officers announced the approach of him whose genius had covered the Army of the Rhine with glory.

Even in that brilliant company, he was easily distinguishable as the hero of the day. He was young and handsome, with a graceful, easy carriage, an air of lofty command, and a mixture of majesty and complaisance in his manner that fitted him to hold sway over those fierce spirits of the Revolution, whom a popular genius alone could control. Dressed in the plain blue uniform of a general, without other decorations than his epaulettes, and mounted on a white steed, which he bestrid with graceful dignity, he wanted neither stars nor golden frippery to mark him for commander.

His courteous bearing and true soldierly gallantry recommended him immediately to O'Hara's heart. To that young enthusiast he appeared at once the ideal republican soldier, without the coarse repulsiveness of the *sans culotte*.

O'Hara was lost in admiration of the gallant young general, when a whisper from Mick Hoolohan drew his attention to another object.

Among the closely-packed crowd that surged around the carriage was one man of peculiarly remarkable appearance. He was one of the very lowest order of the Cordeliers, raggedly dressed, and ill-shaven, but with muscles like iron, and a face of hard, ruthless resolution. Mingled hate and misery glittered in his eye; and his mouth was set with brutal ferocity. He watched the procession go by without moving a muscle or uttering a cheer.

But it was not the man's appearance alone that fixed O'Hara's attention upon him. Just as the staff were approaching, he saw a hand moved cautiously to his breast, and, in the motion that followed, he clearly saw the glitter of a pistol. Every eye being fixed on the gay uniforms, none but O'Hara and his watchful retainer saw the movement. The stories of the early revolution and its sanguinary episodes recurred to O'Hara with painful force. The manner of the man—his stolid coldness, and the resolution written on his hard face—convinced him that he was in presence of an assassin. He awaited the issue with beating heart and watchful eye.

There was no time to be lost. The staff were already abreast of the carriage. The young general was bowing and smiling his acknowledgments of the *vivas* poured upon him. The crowd, intent on the military spectacle, were heedless of aught else. Just as they passed, O'Hara noticed the Cordelier draw his hand from his breast. He was right! It was a pistol, and it was now gleaming without disguise. It was pointed with deadly aim at the general! Another moment, and the heart that had passed unscathed over the battle-fields of La Vendee and Alsace would have been pulseless forever. Quick as lightning O'Hara bounded from the carriage, and threw himself with his full weight on the assassin. The fellow's hand was on the trigger; and, in the collision that followed, it went off. There was a wild shriek from the startled crowd; and, in an instant, thousands were pressing to the spot.

In the first excitement of the struggle O'Hara grappled with his antagonist; but the enraged crowd tore the assassin madly from the grasp of his captor. Then a sickening faintness crept over O'Hara, a burning pain in the arm filled him with agony, everything began to swim around him—he knew that he was wounded. In the misty moments of his dying consciousness he felt himself supported by the gallant young general, whose large, kindly eyes were looking down on him thankfully, while over him bent in anxious tearfulness Lucy Colthurst and her brother. All else he recollected was the ring of sympathetic faces round him, and the murmured hopes and fears, and then the quick ebbing of consciousness as he sank into a trance.

CHAPTER XX.

DEEPENING MYSTERY.

WE return for a while to Glengarra.

On a bleak January evening, a few days after Charles's departure, Milly O'Hara sat alone by the fire in her little boudoir.

She had dismissed even her old faithful nurse for the night, and, with her long hair pillowed on her little snowy hands, she watched the embers flickering and waning.

There was no other light than the fire in the little chamber, which looked vacant and gloomy enough, save in the charmed circle of golden light playing round its lovely mistress.

She was no longer the light-hearted child we have seen her. The revulsion from gayety to grief was even more sensible in contrast with what she had been. Brave she still was—brave enough to think of everything, and to face everything—but altered otherwise from the mirthful girl to the thoughtful woman. And with the pain of the change came over her soul a flood of those sweet, soothing, womanly sympathies that consecrate suffering, and clothe grief in radiant vesture. She almost felt happier, if sadder, in the new character than in the old.

And in the gathering gloom she was thinking—deeply, earnestly thinking—and shaping out thoughts and hopes from among the flickering embers. Where was Charlie?

Did he think of her? Would he ever return? Would they ever, ever again clasp one another to their hearts as in the old, glad time? When, if ever, would the clouds—those dark, pitiless clouds—lift from above Glengarra? When would the Spring time return, or did the Winter of their hopes cover the whole long, weary journey to the grave?

Ah! but the soft flutter of that little heart, the flush over the white face, as her thoughts led her away to other speculations. The broad shoulders and kindly laughing eyes of another absent one perpetually mingled in her thoughts and shared in her hopes—hopes timidly shadowed out, and peopled only by fleeting images.

And then, with a shudder, she turned to thoughts of home, of her father, and of herself. Home! She scarcely recognized it by that name. Stripped of its joys, it seemed rather like a prison than a home to the young soul soaring beyond it.

Poor old Glengarra! It seemed to wear mourning for the desolation of its ancient masters. The park was so cold-looking, the hills so silent, the rooks so mournful in their murmurs, it seemed as if sorrow had blighted all at once the people and the place.

And the house! It had never looked so haggard and chilly before. The wind was always moaning in the huge chambers. The old furniture seemed to have grown a hundred years older and blacker. The servants moved about on tiptoe, as in a house of death.

Ever since his parting with his son, Mr. O'Hara was lost to the world. Through the long hours, and far into the silent nights, he sat gloomily in the cheerless library—stern determination written on his brow—secret repining eating at his heart. Nobody saw the haughty man save his lovely child, who wept for him and caressed him incessantly, and even her he patted and kissed with a fond, regretful sigh, and begged of her to leave him. She dared not even hint at the circumstances that had wrought all this ruin. The frown on his face repulsed spoken sympathy as surely as his awful wasting sorrow provoked it. It was as if a strong will were fighting against earth and heaven, and as if a seeming victory were luring him to destruction. The will never yielded: but the body wasted—the soul wasted slowly, steadily away. And, in her helpless agony, Milly O'Hara dimly perceived the end.

As for Inkston, she had never seen him since the election day. She knew he was in the house, but carefully avoided an interview with him. Somehow she had conceived a strange repugnance to the man, founded not on anything she saw or knew, but on some hidden instinct that taught her to dislike him. His remaining in the house, too, after Charlie had left it, and the suddenness with which their friendship appeared to have been reft, increased her aversion by supplying food for doubts and suspicions, which she yielded to without being able to formulate them.

With such a fever of thoughts throbbing at her poor little brain, Milly was pondering over the flickering embers, her bright black eyes searching the ruddy flames, and her soft pale cheek resting wearily on her snowy white hand.

A light foot-fall on the carpet startled her from her meditations. She looked around hurriedly—a man's form was dimly recognizable.

"Mr. Inkston!" she exclaimed, with not a little asperity.

"Pardon me, Miss O'Hara," he cried, advancing towards her; "I did not intend to interrupt you."

"I am not occupied, sir," said she, in the same cold,

dispassionate voice; "but I thought you knew that this was my private chamber, and that"——

"Yes, yes, Miss O'Hara," he returned, pleadingly, "I have to crave your pardon for my intrusion; but let the circumstances be my justification. I have sought you all through the house in vain, and finding the door open, I unwittingly disturbed you here. I wished to see you to say good-bye."

"Good-bye!"

"Yes; I am leaving Glengarra to-night—perhaps forever—and I could not go away without seeing you."

"Oh! Mr. Inkston, I fear I have been very rude," she cried, her native generosity succeeding to bitterness at sight of his pale, sad face. "Grief does not improve one's manners. Pray be seated."

She lighted a lamp on the mantelpiece, whose flame brought out in deathly hues the handsome, haggard face of the young student. It was wonderfully pale, yet there was something pleadingly sad and mysterious about it that revived all the old fascination. She noted the change with kindred pity.

"I am grieved to say, Mr. Inkston," said she, gently, "that the period of your visit has been so full of unpleasantness to all of us. We have not paid you the attention we should; but I know you are generous enough to forgive us. We have all been sorely tried; poor Charlie's absence has damped our spirits sadly."

"Pray do not pain yourse'f by recalling these sad events," said Inkston, in a low, thrilling voice. "Believe me, my dear Miss O'Hara, not even you can mourn your brother's mishap with a deeper pang than I do."

In her innocence she might have wondered why he had not shown his sympathy more practically; but the almost sepulchral solemnity of his voice awed, while it perplexed her. She had not before noticed those shades of mystery and unhappiness which mingled, now more than ever, with his smiles. They interested her—she could not tell why—probably because they hung like clouds over some tale of mystery, whose colorings were reflected on the veil that concealed it.

"But I have come here," he added, hastily, "to speak to you on other matters than these."

"Indeed!" she exclaimed, somewhat uneasily.

"I have come to say good-bye, and yet I have not the strength to say it."

"Farewells are often painful."

"Yes, Miss O'Hara; but when the farewell means farewell to life and hope—when the farewell is a sentence of life-long misery—then it is hard to say it."

She glanced in amazement at him, and saw a dangerous light in his eyes and a hectic flush on his cheek.

"I cannot imagine what you mean, Mr. Inkston," she said.

"Hear, then, the explanation," he cried, throwing himself passionately at her feet—"I mean that in leaving you I leave my heart, my hope, my life!"

"Mr. Inkston!" she exclaimed, starting back in affright.

"Hear me, and then spurn me if you will," he cried, wildly. "If I surprise you, I do not less surprise myself. I implore your mercy at the same time that I crave your love. Hear me patiently, for heaven's sake," he cried, as she moved towards the door in terror and amaze, "hear a confession that is burning to unfold itself. I love you—how ardently—how absorbingly—how madly — words could not picture. You have drawn me from a shelter whence I had hoped to despise mankind, and have made of me a passionate votary of beauty. Reluctantly, and with many a bitter struggle, I have yielded to the immortal power. It has seized my soul—it has fevered my brain—it has steeped my very blood in madness. All that life could offer—all that death could rob me of—has concentrated in one image. That image is yours. In the depths of your beauty lie mirrored my alternative paths in life. The one leads to bliss unutterable. The other points the way to the grave, and ends in the dark country beyond. Say, say to which you will consign me?"

She listened tremblingly. His wild energy frightened and surprised her.

"Think, think, Mr. Inkston," she said, as gently and collectedly as she could. "You cannot surely expect an answer to so strange an avowal."

"Why strange, when honest?"

"Surely, you have not forgotten that this is a house of grief—that my heart is too full of the troubles of my dearest friends to admit a lighter thought—that a week has not yet passed since my brother left this roof"——

"All, all I recollect—too well."

"Nor can you have forgotten that—that I have seen very little of you. Much less can you have imagined that I have had leisure for love. Have I not said enough in reply to you?"

Instead of decreasing, his ardor was only mounting.

"Yes, yes," he exclaimed, wildly, "you have said enough for reason. But argument with love is as stubble to a furnace. It flames hotter and hotter with such fuel."

"If I cannot, then, appeal to your reason, shall I not to your generosity? If, as you say, you love me, can you not pity me?"

"Alas! love absorbs pity, or calls selfishness in its name. Tell me to die, and I shall do so for your sake—tell me anything, and, if it be the worst of fates, I shall embrace it gladly. But, oh! do not force me to look into the fire of doubt and agony."

"But why press for an answer so suddenly?"

"I leave Glengarra to-night, perhaps forever."

"But why forever?"

The simplicity of the question recalled the dark shadows to his face; but he flung them from him wildly.

"No matter why," he cried. "I may never see you again if you do not bid me see you."

His pertinacity was beginning to incense her.

"I had given you credit, sir," she said, "for more consideration for a woman's feelings."

"If I lack it, blame yourself, sweet enchantress," he cried, passionately; "you have entranced my senses. They move but at the bidding of your love."

"Once more, sir," she said, with increasing resolution, "I appeal to your good sense and generosity to end this unpleasant scene. You are under my father's roof, and I wish to part with you only as a friend."

"Think, think, let me implore of you," he replied, his dark eyes flashing terribly; "I only ask of you one word—one look that would bid me hope. Such love as mine brooks no obstacles. Oh! beware! Do not make me desperate!"

With instant resolution she replied:

"This is too much, sir. As a man, you might have avoided insulting a girl in her own home. Your threats I despise, sir; and for the rest, if you value any opinion I may retain of you, let me beg of you not to provoke me to further remonstrance."

There was more of deep sadness than of resentment in the look with which he received these cutting reproaches. In the very agony of his anguish, he murmured, mournfully:

"O heaven! what have I done, that my cup should be so bitter?"

Then, as if ashamed of his emotion, he collected himself with a fearful effort. He rose from the ground, and turned towards her a face, haggard and ghastly as a corpse.

"Your pardon, Miss O'Hara," he said, in a low, sepulchral voice, "I have been betrayed into saying more than I should. Your answer is sufficiently explicit. Believe me, I shall *try* to forget you. Farewell."

He was gone before she could utter a word. But the pale, pale face, and the strange black eyes haunted her still; and the words, "I shall *try* to forget you," still rang like a funeral knell in her ear.

How the shadows were thickening round Glengarra! How the spirit-voices sounded in the air! How everything seemed weighing on that fair young breast!

CHAPTER XXI.

AWAKING.

When Charles O'Hara recovered consciousness, after his long, long sleep, it was as if some delicious music were stealing over his senses and charming them back to life. It came like a flood of golden water, so calm and soothing on his poor heated brain, refreshing his memory and lulling his troubled thoughts into a sweet composure. He listened with the helpless rapture of a child, while the melody changed to some plaintive air heard long ago in Ireland.

The rich flowing voice of the singer seemed to blend in the wild melody of her harp, rising softly, like the music of her land, from depths of pensive sadness, welling up from the soul with passionate tenderness, until it burst into a chant of almost defiant hope.

As the voice died away in a heavenly whisper the invalid raised himself with a cry of joy. He fell back in helpless agony.

In an instant a sylph-like form was by his side. Those dreamy, heavenly eyes were looking down into his, and he sank calmly to rest, supported on her snowy bosom.

When he woke again, it was with a sensation of unutterable bliss, for there were kisses on his fevered brow, and SHE was still looking down on him like a guardian angel.

"Dear Charlie, are you better?" she inquired in a

low, musical voice, as she brushed the long hair from his hot face.

"Lucy!" was all that he could say, looking up at her still in charmed wonderment.

"There, there, do not exert yourself," she whispered, stroking his pillow softly. "You will be better directly."

He obeyed her like a child, and glided into a refreshing slumber, whence he awoke to find her yet at his side. She handed him some cooling drink, which he swallowed thirstily, and found himself much stronger.

"Where am I?" he asked, mechanically surveying the chamber. It was charmingly neat, and even luxurious, in its appointments, and looked out on pleasant gardens. The sun was streaming through the open window, bringing with it the odor of sweet flowers and the fresh bracing air of spring.

"Hush! dear!" she whispered. "You are at home."

And home had never seemed so blissful to him as at that moment.

"How long have I been here?" he again asked, after a pause.

"Oh! very long. You have been very near dying. The arm has not been amputated, but you have had a terrible six-weeks' fever."

He looked up again wonderingly into her face, and saw how pale and weary it was. He dimly thought what those six weeks were to his watchful angel.

"Dear Lucy! And you have been with me!" he murmured in feeble rapture.

"Dear, dear Charlie!" she cried, impulsively, kissing his parched lips. "There now, do not speak. You are too weak yet."

"Oh! no, I am quite strong now," said he, at the same time sensible of a burning pain in the arm and an

utter helplessness at contradiction with his words.
"Do, Lucy, do tell me who was he—he that—that was
so near being killed."

"O, Charlie!" she cried, glowingly, "you have saved
the noblest life in all France. It was Hoche!"

"Hoche!"

"Yes, yes, the bravest soldier of the Republic."

"And this is his house?"

"It is: and your home. Since your sickness not a
day has passed that he did not watch for hours by your
bedside. But, see! Here he comes himself."

The door was opened softly, and he of the Rue St.
Honore, only in plain undress, glided noiselessly to the
bedside.

"O, General, he is awake." cried Miss Colthurst, pressing his hand.

"Thank heaven!" murmured the soldier, earnestly.
Then bending over the sufferer, he took his pallid hand
and passed his own softly over the throbbing temples.
"How now, my deliverer?" he asked gently. "Death
has not been so cruel as to rob me of the delight of
thanking you."

O'Hara smiled faintly.

"You have been very ill though," continued the General. "It is quite a miracle you have not lost an arm.
You were happy to have so fair a nurse as *la-belle Lucie*."

"Nonsense, General," said the blushing girl. "You
are but concealing your own good deeds. But some
other time for congratulations—our poor invalid is too
weak to listen to our prattle."

"Very true, sweet one," said Hoche. "Thoughtful
as ever. *Eh bien!* I shall leave him for a while in your
custody. To-morrow, Mr. O'Hara, you will be more
robust to receive my rude thanks."

"Mercy! it is Jack!" cried Miss Colthurst in alarm, as a heavy footstep sounded in the passage.

He was in the room, and by the bedside, before her whisper could stop him.

"Why, Charlie, alive again, old boy, eh?" he cried, in his big, jolly voice, enfolding the languid hand of the sufferer in his huge palm.

"Dear Jack, recollect that he is not quite as strong as a lion yet," interposed Miss Colthurst.

"Humbug, Lucy, child, humbug!" he retorted, beaming down on his sick friend with his great kindly eyes. "'Tis n't Charlie O'Hara is there if a Tipperary shake hands disagrees with his nerves. Eh, Charlie?"

The pleased glow on the invalid's face was a satisfactory answer. There was life in the clutch of that great honest hand.

"I knew it, old boy," ran on Colthurst, triumphantly. "The girls are all very well to smoothe a fellow's way to the other world, but, St. Patrick! give me the grip of a Tipperary man to bring him back again. Never mind, Charlie. We'll dance a *moneen* on the Galtees yet, old fellow! The General here is a mighty fine hand at the bagpipes; and 'tis the devil's own case if the Sassenach don't pay the piper. There, there, Lucy, I'm not going to ask him to fight a duel or win an Irish election, though people can do that same. Eh? old boy! By all that's wonderful, you're more of a man again this minute than Lucy made you for the last six weeks."

"*Sacré!* Jack, how you are wonderful!" exclaimed Hoche, as he saw the electric effect of the speaker's good humor on the face of the patient.

"*Magragha!* General, an Irishman for it," was the reply. "'T is the boast of my life that I made a blacksmith down in our country rattle off the chorus of

'Peggy Malone and I,' and he dying of a thundering fever the same night. Fact, faith, General—if ever you have occasion to go to the cross-roads at Kilsheelan, he's there to this day, able to thrash any three Frenchmen of my acquaintance. But, I'm hanged if that isn't Mick Hoolohan. If he once got inside, we'd never get him out, so I think the sooner we're off the better. Keep up the spirits, Charlie—Lucifer fell out of paradise in a fit of low spirits, mind. Take care you don't go too far, though, and run away with Lucy here before you're able to use your sword-arm on her big brother."

Yet, for all his buoyant spirits, Charles O'Hara felt unutterably happier when all were gone again but Lucy, and when he could again rest his weary head on her bosom, and sink into delicious dreams, with her heavenly eye following him into dreamland, and her soft, silken tresses fanning his fevered cheek.

CHAPTER XXII

DOLCE DOLORE.

THERE is nothing in life more tranquilly pleasant than recovery from some prostrating sickness. The lull of memory—the delicious sense of feebleness without pain—the buoyancy with which the elastic frame in health and strength—the bright colors of a new existence, enhanced by contrast with the dull monotony of the sick room—all combine to smooth the way to convalescence.

But doubly dear to Charles O'Hara were the days of his slow recovery, for they were brightened by the companionship of her whose mild seraphic beauty had captivated his heart.

Circumstances threw them almost entirely together. General Hoche, with the honors of La Vendee and Alsace fresh upon him, was at the time the foremost soldier in the service of the republic. Already his pupil and subsequent rival, Napoleon Bonaparte, had signalized himself from among the mob of generals; and there were not wanting suspicions that the young Corsican was one of the instigators of the assassin of the Rue St. Honore. But as yet the hero of La Vendee was chief in the republican councils. His arduous duties in those stormy times carried him away for the major portion of his time to Paris; while Captain Colthurst, not unmindful of his mission, was daily occupied in the intrigues carried on by Wolfe Tone with the republican directory.

Charles O'Hara and Lucy were thus left to their own resources to beguile the time—no difficult task for "two souls with but a single thought—two hearts that beat as one."

Hoche's suburban chateau was situate amid the undulating woods and bosky retreats of Meudon, far away from the noisy strife of the city. The house itself was furnished with republican simplicity. But nature did for its *entourage* what a stiff-necked puritanism had interdicted to art. For miles around, the country was dotted with gentle slopes, beautifully wooded, and bright patches of verdure dipping into crystal lakelets. In the far distance, the towers and steeples of Paris rose against the sky. Nearer, there were gardens, shining fountains, statues, parterres of flowers, leafy arbors, and sequestered walks.

The April flowers were springing up like diamonds on the sward, April dews were on the leaves, and April's radiance in the sky, and the April songsters were tuning their vernal roundelays among the trees.

With a goddess to vivify all this frame-work of romance, Charles O'Hara lived in an atmosphere of bliss during the first stage of his recovery. Breakfast in the fresh rosy morning—out with his fair nurse in the sunny forenoon—siesta in the woods with the loveliest of wood-nymphs—evening calmly, religiously happy—days melted into nights, and nights glided into days, as in a dream of fairyland.

But too quickly—all too quickly! For Charles O'Hara shortly discovered that, as he gained strength, the attentions of Lucy Colthurst relaxed visibly. The maiden blushes on her cheek might have told ordinary observers the obvious tale, that a handsome young fellow in health did not require the same delicate offices she had cheerfully undertaken when he was chained to a bed of sickness. But O'Hara saw only through the deceptive spectacles of love. He saw only that day by day she was more and more divorced from him—that she spoke to him less tenderly and less frequently—that she blushed when he addressed her—that she replied constrainedly—and that she studiously avoided the occasions of those caressings which had aided so much his return to life and vigor.

First came regret, deep and poignant, at the change; then astonishment. In the passion-garden of love, astonishment creeps over the palings that enclose the noisome stalks of jealousy; and Charles O'Hara was not long in overleaping the partition. How the foul poison spreads, dropping like an acid on the velvet petals of affection, feeding on their violet beauty, tainting their myrrhic fragrance, and withering them into shrivelled weeds!

Once the dark spot appeared, abundance of fuel supplied itself to its scorching flame.

With Lucy's estrangement from himself O'Hara now combined her intimacy with Hoche. Through one cause or other, he had taken it for granted that the Colthursts knew the General only through the affair of the Rue St. Honore, and having neglected to make inquiries, he marvelled at the affectionate intercourse that took place between them. A little calm reflection might have shown him how easy and informal that intercourse; but again he blinded himself pettishly to all but the fact that Lucy and Hoche were on the tenderest terms. Hoche seemed, indeed, rather old to captivate a girl of nineteen; but he was good-looking, affable, and loveable, not only for his name, but for his private character.

Reflections such as these made him moody and unhappy; he treated everyone with a cold show of indifference, and withdrew more and more into his own gloomy thoughts.

The vicious charm was not slow to work out its unholy spell. Coldness begat coldness; and with every succeeding day the gulf between Lucy and her lover dilated, until the hallowed bond of affection seemed nearly snapped. With Hoche, too, he became rude and unpleasing; while he even credited Jack with participation in the conspiracy against him.

Unhappiness was establishing itself firmly in the chateau. The spring, the flowers, the birds, everything ministered to its melancholy sway.

One day wrapt, up in his morbid meditations, Charles O'Hara had strayed from the gardens out into the neighboring wood, whose gloomiest depths he pierced in the hope of hiding his sorrows there.

Suddenly he came from behind on a little artificial arbor overlooking a pretty lake among the trees. He was turning away, when a sob, a low, anguished whisper, striking to his very heart, arrested his steps.

A smarting pain shot through his frame. He stood as if smitten by lightning. That low cry of grief had startled the brooding nest of suspicion.

He advanced slowly and cautiously. A few steps more, and he saw through the foliage a sight that thrilled his every vein.

Lucy Colthurst was seated within the arbor, her head resting on her hands, in a posture of profoundest grief. Her long auburn tresses, escaping under the little hat, flowed carelessly around her. Her face was bedewed with tears, and her beautiful eyes, red with weeping, were raised to heaven with angelic fervor.

O'Hara watched her with fascinated attention. The silent eloquence of her grief stirred every feeling of his heart, and clothed them again in their olden garb of enthusiastic warmth. He had never pictured to himself so fair a creature laden with dolors. At one rush the streams of love flowed again over his soul, and swept away every vestige of jealousy, leaving only the clinging sense of humiliation and shame.

He did everything by impulse, and a new impulse was on him now.

Before he could think or control himself he was on his knees at her feet; and as he looked up appealingly into her tearful face he cried: "Lucy! Lucy! can you forgive me?"

Her first thought—startled and surprised—was to fly; but she was detained by his earnest, imploring prayer. She could only turn away her head, and hide her face in her hands.

"Hear me, Lucy," he cried passionately, seizing her unresisting hand. "You have much to pardon me; but, oh! believe me, it was only my love for you that blinded me. Your recent coldness towards me, the way you seemed to avoid me—shall I confess it?—your intimacy with General Hoche, all have soured my temper and betrayed my better judgment. Blind fool that I was! I thought you had ceased to love me—that you had transferred your heart to another. Blame only my love, dearest Lucy, and let my constancy in the future atone for my cruel, stupid jealousy."

He spoke with all the fervency he was capable of, and kissed the white hand that lay in his as token of his repentance.

A sudden light seemed to dawn upon her. She wiped her tears away hastily, and looked at the suppliant at her feet.

"I fear," said she, "we have both been victims of a cruel mistake. Can it be possible that you have mistaken the affection between my uncle and me for love?"

"Your uncle!"

"Oh! stupid," she cried, "that we have never told you before."

"But, General Hoche, surely he is——"

"My mother's brother," was the reply. "He is living in Paris only during the war—his wife and family are in Bretagne."

"Oh! this is too ludicrous," said O'Hara, almost laughing at the *contretemps*. "Surely, dearest Lucy, if anything were wanting to make my penance complete, it would be my laughable predicament at the present moment. I scarcely know whether your anger or your ridicule would be more cruel on me."

"No, no," said Lucy, smiling sweetly through her tears; "I am myself much to blame for omitting to tell you this; but then, it never occurred to me for a moment that you did not know."

"Oh! who but a brute, as I am, need be told so," cried O'Hara. "Dearest Lucy, can you forget my lunatic suspicions?"

"Nay, Charlie," she returned, with a smile, "I am going to relieve you of part of your burden. I confess that your coldness made me unhappy—made me half fear that——"

"Darling!" he exclaimed, interrupting her, as she made a confession which fairly enchanted him, "you only enkindle my rage at my own stupidity."

"Then shall we not forget it?" she asked, looking up trustfully into his sparkling blue eyes.

"Not so, dearest," said O'Hara, with a smile; "I intend to do ample penance, and will this very night tell Hoche that I had mistaken him for an Abelard of nineteen; ay, and even bear Jack's laugh with perfect equanimity. But, bless you! dearest Lucy, you have indeed lifted a weight off my heart."

"The service has not been disinterested, then," said she, with a blush. "O Charlie, it seems like new life to me, that we are happy together again."

And the old blissful dream wafted them once more into the fairy courts of love, and they marvelled all the more delightfully at the sapphire walls, and drank all the more refreshingly at the golden fountains, because a blind chance had so nearly closed them for ever against them.

And unflinchingly, Charles O'Hara related the whole story of his love and jealousy to Hoche and Jack Colthurst. And the home circle at the chateau was once more undimmed.

Henceforth, the lovers were, so to say, almost wholly wrapt up in one another. They spent the long sunny days roaming the woods and flowery meadows together. They followed the fortunes of some hero and heroine of Spanish or Italian romance, or talked of nature's loveliness, or, gazing into one another's eyes, spoke the pure, unsyllabled language of love. In the evenings, their wedded music followed the sun, like airy cherubim, in his progress through the west—that west where Ireland lay sleeping—and in the starlit night they still peered through the silvery windows of the sky into that resplendent far, far away country, where love issues from the dazzling throne of the Godhead.

CHAPTER XXIII.

NEWS FROM HOME.

CHARLES O'HARA had spent over a month in cloudless happiness after his recovery, when one morning, before he was awake, Mick Hoolohan tore into the room, shouting wildly:

"Masther Charles! Masther Charles!"

"In heaven's name, man, have you gone mad?" demanded O'Hara, starting half-asleep from a delightful slumber.

"Divil a bit, Masther Charles," cried Mick, handing his master a closely sealed letter. "You may cut me up for ould turf if that isn't Miss Milly's handwritin'. My own little darlin'! I wondher how they're all at home. Whillilew! ould Glengarra an' Tipperary for ever! There's nothin' like it here, for all their chatter and big dhrums!"

While Mick galloped on in his patriotic reflections, O'Hara greedily tore, and recognized, with delight, his sister's handwriting. He had written to her immediately on his recovery; but as postal communication between France and England was at the time interrupted, he was forced to commit his letter to a more uncertain vehicle, and scarcely hoped it would ever reach its destination.

A thousand memories weighing on his brain, he

glanced eagerly through the welcome missive. The tale it told will be best given in the words of the writer:

"Glengarra, April, ——.

"MY DEAR, DEAR BROTHER,—I have received your precious note, and now gladly seize an opportunity of writing to you. Oh! Charlie, I have so much to tell you—such a load of sorrow to unfold to you, that I almost hesitate to break in on your happiness, by making you a sharer of my confidence. But you will pardon me, I know, my own dear brother, when you reflect that I have now no one in the world to confide in but you. I am very, very much changed, Charlie. You would hardly know me for what I was. But I have still, I trust, a brave heart, and I am sustained by the blessed confidence that heaven will one day or other bring us together again in happiness.

"I have so much to tell you, I hardly know where to begin. You will make allowances for my distracted state of mind. Well, then, to commence. I shall not trouble you by telling how utterly miserable I felt after our last sad parting. Let us forget that, and look to a happier *reunion*. For days after you left, I could do nothing but weep, and try to console poor papa; but he never, never would let me speak of you, though I know your memory is burning his poor broken heart.

"Fancy, then, my surprise—shall I say indignation?—in the midst of my grief, to receive from your—oh! I cannot call him, friend—Inkston, a declaration of love! I never could like the man—he was such a dark, strange puzzle; but as he was in my father's house, I tried to show him how unreasonable and misplaced his affection was. Oh! you should have seen how terrible he looked! We parted in anger; but I knew instinctively we had not parted forever.

"That very night he left Glengarra. Before he went he had a strange interview with poor papa. What passed between them I cannot guess; but it must have been something terrible and mysterious, for, when I went down afterwards to bid papa good-night, he seemed nearly out of his mind. Oh! dear Charlie! such a weight of sorrow as seeemed to be pressing him down, down to the earth! And he kissed me so passionately, and then became so fierce and cold again, I knew that horrid stranger had struck a new wound into his heart.

"But that was only the beginning of my trouble. The next day, while musing lonelily in the garden, I was accosted by Inkston's servant, James—a being, if possible, more mysterious than himself. The man approached me with reverence, and I knew from his strange manner of interest that he was on no unfriendly mission. His words are engraven on my heart as clearly as I now transcribe them to you.

"'Lady,' he said, in a broken foreign accent, 'I come to warn you that you are in danger. My master intends to carry you off. His plan is to seize you alone in your evening walk to-morrow. I am to have a carriage in waiting at the west park gate. I have joined my master to aid him in revenge, but I cannot assist him in a crime. Therefore, I warn you, dear lady. I only make one condition—that my master shall not be injured.'

"Can I tell you my feelings on learning this news? Oh! no, they were too confused and terrible. But Heaven sustained me, and my courage did not desert me. I sent for Joe Hogan, the Captain of the Rovers, who has already befriended me when most I needed his help. I determined that Inkston should be taught a lesson once for all. Poor Joe was, of course, ardent in my service. We arranged that I should take my walk as usual, that Joe should have three of his men in readiness to assist me at the first call, and that I should then meet my enemy and denounce him.

"I will pass over my troubled thoughts in the meantime. You will understand me when I say that I was not dismayed. I was there at the usual hour, and so was he. He renewed to me the most fervent protestations of love, and, if love were a mere passionate adoration, I believe he spoke truly. He besought of me not to tempt him into a course at which his love revolted, though his passion drove him on.

"Wearied at last by his importunity, I reproached him, perhaps too severely, for talking of love to me, whom he was at that moment plotting to decoy into a fate worse than death. My words seemed to sting him to madness. He approached as if to seize me. I drew back, and gave the signal agreed on with the Rover. In an instant my four gallant protectors sprang on the path.

"Inkston was stunned, but wonderfully cool—dark, hideous shadows crept over his white face; and I thought he looked more like a handsome demon than a man as he whispered in my ear:

"'This, then, is a trap, fair lady. Be it so: you have the victory. But think not I yield you to the threats of yonder assassins. I might even face the four of them, but that my mission is not yet accomplished. I am now doubly venomed for revenge. Farewell! we shall meet again. Farewell!'

"Before I could recover from the pain of his hot, cruel words, he had disappeared through the grove; and I have not seen him since.

"Dear, dear Charlie, I feel assured that that man is a deadly enemy of our house. I feel he is at the root of all our sorrows. But I have not yet told you the heaviest grief of all. Since Inkston left the house, darling papa has grown worse and worse. For a long time he refused to see anyone, and locked himself up in the dreary library, always grieving, and such an awful deadly grief! Then his health gave way, and now he is stretched on a bed of sickness, from which I fear he will never rise, unless to go to heaven. Dearest Charlie, my tears blot what I am writing. I scarcely know how to tell you how ghastly he has got, and how white his hair has grown.

"Dearest, fondest brother, I implore of you to forget what has passed, and to return home while there is yet time to make his death happy. Ah! if you only knew how he loves you, and how grief for your absence is eating away his heart. I know that if you returned you would bend his proud heart! Sorrow has nearly worn away his sullen obstinacy, and he has grown so accustomed to caressing me, and seems so happy when I am with him, that I never leave his bedside. Oh! I know that if his rosy little favorite, Charlie, were once more by his side, he would leave this world with a happy soul.

"Besides, my own darling brother, I implore you to come for my sake. I fear to be alone in this now deserted house. I am sure that Inkston has not abandoned his vile plots against me, and I almost dread to commit myself to the protection of the outlaw captain. Poor Joe! I know that he would lose his life for me; but he loves me so much that—— I hardly know what to say, but that I would be brave and happy once more if I had you by my side. Think, then, of my defenceless condition, and of poor darling papa, and I know you will come to us.

"Give my warmest love to Lucy and Jack Colthurst. Dear Charlie, you ought to love her, for she is an angel. Tell Jack I miss him sadly. Once more, darling Charlie, receive the most affectionate love and deepest blessings of
"Your loving sister,
"MILLY."

CHAPTER XXIV.

PARTING.

ONE thought alone possessed O'Hara on reading his sister's letter—to return at all hazards and immediately to Glengarra. Overwhelmed with grief at the terrible pass to which his family had been brought, he descended into the breakfast-room, as in a dream.

Lucy Colthurst was there before him, and alone. She tripped up to greet him as usual, but started back, he looked so pale and sorrowful.

"Why, Charlie, dear, what *has* happened?" she asked in a tone of deep concern.

Without a word, he handed her the letter. She devoured it eagerly, and was in tears before she had perused it.

"Oh! go, dearest Charlie, go immediately!" she cried, after reading it.

"My own dearest Lucy, I knew you would say so. Yes—I will go immediately. We must part for the present, dearest. Our dream of happiness was too fair for this world."

"Nay, dearest Charlie, our happiness would be misery while poor Milly is so wretched."

"Lucy, you are an angel," he said; "I had thought my heaviest grief would be my parting with you, and now I find it is my lightest and sweetest duty."

"Dear Charlie, could I hesitate?" she asked, looking

up lovingly into his face. "I shall willingly bear my share of poor dear Milly's sorrow. Go, Charlie—we have heaven to sustain us."

"Yes, dearest, and the hope that our parting shall be but for awhile."

"And that our hearts will still be joined, though the sea divides us."

"Heaven bless you, darling!" he returned, "I am now strong against all the world's buffets. But here comes Jack."

Around the breakfast-table the little circle discussed Miss O'Hara's letter, and but one advice came from all sides—that Charles should set out without delay to his sister's assistance.

"But I cannot go," said O'Hara, "without at least doing something for the mission on which I came. I fear my happiness here has blinded me to everything but my own gratification."

"It must be, then, that I am to blame," said Hoche, with a smile, "for I have given you the excuse of being an invalid. But make your mind at rest on that point—our friend Jack has done wonders with the Directory."

"And very little I've got for my pains," put in Colthurst; "poor Tone is wearing out his life in trying to bring them to reason."

"True, true!" said Hoche, sadly. "I have often thought they are insincere in their dealings with your countrymen. The truth is, Carnot is the Directory, and Carnot thinks of nothing but of placing Germany under the yoke. He despises England."

"My soul, then, he's making a great mistake!" blurted out Colthurst.

"I have always thought so," pursued the general. "France has to fear England alone, and England can only be struck through Ireland. I told them this over and over, yet they seem not to heed it. Time may bring them a more bitter teacher."

"Do you, then, despair, General, of French aid to Ireland?" asked O'Hara.

"*Sacre*, no. Time works wonders. Tone is an able advocate, and our friend Jack is one of the types the most astonishing of Irishmen—so *grand* and persuasive."

"And to give them their due," put in Colthurst, "Barras and the rest of them are not a bad sort of fellows."

"There is still hope, then, in a continuance of the negotiations?"

"*Ma foi!* yes. I love Ireland much. It shall go hard with me if I do not come across you in your Dublin in a little time. But—let me see—I go to the Luxembourg myself this morning to consult with the Directory. What if you come with me? I may give you some news to encourage our Irish friends."

"Many thanks, General," said O'Hara, "I accept your offer with pleasure. It will be at least something to bring home with me the latest report of our prospects with the Directory."

Accordingly, the three lost no time in setting out for the city.

Getting out on the boulevards, they noticed signs of unusual commotion. In the streets leading to the Palace of the Luxembourg, where the Directory sat, the excitement was still more intense; and when they entered the square fronting the palace, they found their passage blocked by an inhumerable and motley crowd.

Men in all sorts of uniforms were there—National Guards, with their rifles—women from the garrets of the faubourgs—men in blouses—ragged urchins—all commingled in a motley, excited multitude, gesticulating in groups, shouting, chattering, and pushing. The faces of the crowd showed that something disastrous had happened—they spoke in excited whispers—and there was mingled rage and revenge pictured in their looks.

In the great entrance hall of the palace were collected groups of officers of all arms, conversing as excitedly as those outside, who saluted the General gravely while he passed.

"Something has occurred!" whispered Hoche, as he mounted the great staircase with his two friends.

The passages were lined with officers, and there were sentries at every corner. Striking into one of the corridors, he led his companions into an ante-chamber, where he bid them await his return.

"Some bad news must have arrived," he said. "People never look grave here unless the war goes badly. The Directory will be awaiting me."

They were detained for more than an hour, the while the confusion in the palace and the uneasy murmurs of popular disappointment reached their ears to increase their suspense.

While chafing at the delay, Hoche himself entered, looking agitated and depressed.

"Ah! dear friends, sad news—sad news," he said. "The Army of the Rhine has been forced to retreat before the Austrians, and Moreau has abandoned all his positions. I am ordered to set out two hours hence to take command of the army of the Meuse. The position is a very critical one; but I know we shall be able to out-general those Austrians."

"Then the Irish scheme is definitely abandoned," asked O'Hara.

"For the present, yes. But the German campaign cannot last long. Once back to Paris, the invasion of

Ireland shall be my first care. Tell Ireland I pledge myself to her redemption."

"Enough, General," cried O'Hara, warmly. "May heaven prosper your arms in the meantime!"

"I am almost tempted to follow you, General," cried Colthurst; "I should like dearly to strike for the republic again—but for Lucy's sake and for Ireland's."

"Tut, tut, Jack," interposed the General. "For both their sakes you must stay in Paris."

"Well, well, be it so," said Colthurst, discontentedly. "If we don't have a fight in Germany, we'll have one in Ireland one of those days."

And so they parted—the one on his way to an early grave—the others—but we may not anticipate.

CHAPTER XXV.

THE BROKEN OAK.

It was night—a cheerless, unnatural summer night—when Charles O'Hara reached Glengarra.

The tall trees in the park beat time to his thoughts with their melancholy rustle. The rambling old mansion looked gaunt and grave in its ivy pall. All was so dark and woe-begone, so eloquent with mystic emblems of grief—like a mourning shadow, where the Glengarra of his young days had stood.

He hurried past with a heavy heart. Once in the house he felt he was in the companionship of death. The servants moved about like shadows in the subdued light, speaking in whispers. The lofty halls and passages seemed never so lonely before. A chill wind crept through the corridors, where everything was so vacant and dark. At every footfall sounded the echo of the great destroyer's tread.

His hopes crushed and broken, O'Hara traversed the empty halls. And now his guide, stopping before one of the doors, motioned to him silently, and then glided away

Did he think, as he turned the muffled handle, of that other moment, a few months since, when he stood on the self-same threshold, awaiting the stern sentence of an iron-willed man? Ah! no—for the white face pillowed on the couch told him that the iron will was broken, and

THE CLOUDLAND OF LIFE.   215

the strong frame hurrying to decay. And the choking tide of sorrows, welling up from his heart, drowned every record of that old man's life, save his sacred name of father.

In the dim light of the sick room two figures knelt by the bedside—the one, a white-haired priest, the other a pale, pale girl. A deathly solemnity was there.

Light as was the footstep of the intruder, the watchers turned from their devotions. One moment, and the fair girl by the bedside was clinging to O'Hara's neck, and brother and sister met once more.

"What hope?" was all he could ask through his blinding tears.

She shook her head, and drew him gently towards the bedside.

"None in this world," she whispered. "You have come only to see the end."

"Is there yet time?" he again asked.

"Yes, yes," she whispered, "time enough yet to rob death of its bitterness."

As they spoke, the sound of voices seemed to waken the sleeper. A face, wonderfully pale, now no longer seamed with the iron furrows of grief, but, as it were, smoothed out for the last great reckoning, moved on the pillow.

His eyes opened slowly, wearily, as though already far advanced to the darkness of the grave.

They wandered to the bedside—opened wider. A vision of the past was before them now, like a delusive dream.

A terrible convulsion shook his frame—he started wildly from the couch—that vision was there again—nearer—nearer. A strong arm encircled his neck—two brimming eyes looked down into his.

The vision was a reality, and father and son were

locked in one another's arms in the pale light of death's ghastly lamp.

Why intrude upon a scene so solemn with the cold mockery of words? The demon of pride had at last forsaken his victim, and the radiant angels of love took his place in the clear cold shadow of death.

The divine potion of forgiveness had drowned the memories of evil days. The pact of absolution was sealed over the grave.

They knelt by the bedside—son and daughter—and a father's blessing, couched in the impressive language of the tomb, shed a halo of sanctity and love around them.

"Father, dear father!" said O'Hara, "may we not be happy yet together?"

The old man smiled feebly and sadly.

"No, no, my son," he said; "the happiness of this world is not for me."

"But, father, have you not anything to tell us—anything of the terrible grief that has eaten away your health and strength?"

A shadow of the old grief darkened the white face, but it disappeared again.

"Come closer to me, my children," said the old man, his voice getting more and more feeble with every ebbing moment; "I have much to tell you, but I am getting weak—very weak."

He shuddered visibly—the cold hand of death was quickly fastening upon him. Milly kissed the ebbing life back again to his cheeks.

"Listen, Charlie!" he whispered, in a weak, trembling voice. "Listen! I would warn you."

"Dear father, I am all attention."

"You know that—that young man—him you call Inkston?"

"Yes, yes, father; what of him?"

"Beware of him—beware of him!" said the dying man, with a shudder. "He is my enemy—and yours—beware of him!"

"But why? Who is he, father? What do you know of him?" asked O'Hara, eagerly.

Another fearful shudder convulsed the sinking frame, and the sufferer raised his cold hand feebly to his brow.

"Seek not to know!" he cried. "Seek not to know! Let the secret die with me."

"But might we not console you, father, if it is anything that troubles you?"

"Troubles me!" cried the old man, with a transitory gleam of energy. "It has troubled and tortured every moment of my life for above twenty years. But it will trouble me no longer now—no longer."

He leant back feebly, and his eyes closed, as if he would say no more.

They knelt again by the bedside, and the mournful litany of the dying sounded like funeral bells through the chamber.

Then the dying man raised himself again wearily, and noticed them to come nearer.

"Beware of *him!*" he repeated, solemnly. "Beware of *him!* If you ever meet him, tell him that I have suffered—that I alone am guilty. Tell him a heart of adamant has been torn asunder by grief. Tell him—tell him—that—that I forgive him, as I hope *she* has forgiven me. Enough, my darling children. Heaven bless you! I am going to a better world. God will bless you both in this. Remember what a life of misery has taught me—the strongest cannot battle alone against the world."

There was silence again in the chamber of death. The iron frame was lowered, never to rise again. The eyes wandered away to the darksome future. The soul fluttered, sighed, vanished to its eternal home.

Death was at last the victor!

And the murmurings through the house, and the rustling of the trees, set to a strange mystic music the dead man's legacy—"The strongest cannot battle alone against the world."

CHAPTER XXVI.

THE SIGNAL OF REVOLUTION.

IT was the next day, and all was silence in the house of death. Closeted alone with the dead were Charles O'Hara and his sister, praying, grieving and thinking. A solemn hush was over the house, and the bright summer day was chastened to a dim light, ere it pierced the sombre curtains.

Peace was there at last; and the besetting sorrow of their house seemed banished to another world with the spirit which provoked it.

While wrapt in his meditations a servant softly opened the door, and touched O'Hara on the shoulder.

"A man is below, sir, and wants to see you," he whispered.

"Me! I cannot see anybody now."

"He says he must see you, sir—that his business won't bear a moment's delay."

"Who is the man? Did he give you his name?"

"No, sir; but I think it is 'the Captain' himself."

"What should he want with me?"

"I don't know, sir; he did not say. But he said that you'd understand—that it was 'The Signal.'"

"Great Heaven! is it possible!" cried O'Hara starting from his seat; then checking himself, he turned to the servant. "Where is he? I shall go and see him!"

He found the grim Captain of the outlaws awaiting him in an ante-room, muffled up in the heavy costume which he affected as an addition to his dignity and mystery.

The outlaw approached him without salutation, and whispered some words in his ear. O'Hara started back as if smitten by lightning.

"What! to-night?" he exclaimed, growing pale as death.

"Yes, to-night!" said the outlaw, solemnly.

O'Hara hid his face in his hands for a few moments, as if crushed by the weight of his thoughts. When he looked up again he was collected and resolute.

"Perhaps, after all, it is as well now," said he, in a calm tone. "Death in any shape will be no stranger to me. Yes, issue the orders without delay."

"To-night, then, at the rising of the moon, in the Trooper's Glen?"

"Yes. Let every one be there on pain of death. This last effort must be a supreme one. Heaven grant it may be for the better!"

"It can't be for the worse," murmured the outlaw, hoarsely.

"Well, well, I hope so. What are your other orders?"

"To encamp in the glen for the night. At noon tomorrow another envoy from Dublin should be here. If he is, we march to Kilkenny without delay."

"Thank God, then, I can unite love and duty," cried O'Hara fervently. "Here's how I shall manage, Joe. You will see to all the preparations for to-night; my father shall be buried at daybreak in the morning, and I shall then be at liberty to join you."

"'T will do well," said the outlaw. "We'll have a noble gathering."

"Success, then!" cried O'Hara. "May Heaven bless the cause! For the present, farewell!"

As the broad shadows of evening fell on the hills,

signs of uneasiness broke momentarily on the view. Men were hurrying towards the mountains from all the *sheilings* dotting the plain, and women and children were at the cabin doors in attitudes of speechless supplication.

Then a bright light shot up from the summit of Slieve-na-mon, and from hill to hill the red beacons extended, until the heavens were ablaze with flickering fires.

When the moon rose over the mountains, and stole down in white streams to the Trooper's Glen, there was the tramp of men amid the groves, and there were watchfires glimmering through the glen, and on the silent night air the sound of many voices and the clashing of weapons.

In the dim light of the mourning chamber, Charles O'Hara sat musing still by the side of his dead father. White and peaceful was the face peeping ghostlily out from the shroud in the coffin. Almost as white the fair face of the girl who bent down over it in the last sad moments of their earthly communion.

Out from Clonmel that same moonlight night rode a party of horsemen, whose glittering accoutrements shone in the bright light. They were a yeomanry corps, raised in the neighborhood. At their head rode a dashing-looking cavalier, whose white face, dark hair, and keen flashing eyes looked terrible beneath his burnished casque.

And now the troop halted by a grove on an elevation overlooking Glengarra, as it lay like a huge mausoleum against the silver moon.

The men dismounted, and scattered through the grove; but far into the night their white-faced captain stood gazing intently down into the valley—down where the feeble light was struggling from the house of death!

CHAPTER XXVII.

THE DEATH STRUGGLE.

At break of day, on the morning following the meeting in the Trooper's Glen, a quiet *cortege* left Glengarra, and carried away from it forever its whilom lord.

In the imperfect light there was something sympathetically lonely and sad about the house and park, which seemed like mourners round the bier of their dead master.

The unexpected outbreak of the insurrection, and the position it consequently placed him in, made Charles O'Hara anxious to avoid all display at his father's funeral.

The coffin was laid on a plain bier. The priest in his simple robes preceded the funeral carriage, and behind it walked the heir of Glengarra, with a few of the more intimate friends and retainers of the family. What a contrast to the endless processions and lordly displays usually associated with the burial of an O'Hara!

The cemetery was situate on the confines of the demesne, and was a wild overgrown place, where tall nettles and dense clumps of underwood roamed incontinently over the tombs, and matted themselves with the long switch-grass among the graves, which lay thick and unordered all round. Even the family vault of the O'Haras, unopened till now for over half a century, partook of the general desolation and ruin of the place.

Around the open tomb, in the gray light of morning, were collected the little group of mourners. Charles

O'Hara knelt beside the coffin, while the good old priest intoned the solemn requiem prayers, and the little band of worshippers sent up their murmured orisons to the Most High.

Anon the sacred service was concluded, and amid a whispered prayer the coffin was lowered into the tomb. To such humble limits had come the haughty lord of Glengarra!

Charles O'Hara was gazing into the pit to which all that was mortal of his father was retreating, and the workmen were already closing the grave, when a loud clatter of horses' hoofs on the road outside jarred strangely with the solemn hush within.

With common impulse the mourners looked up from he grave, to see a horseman dismount at the graveyard gate, and run towards them in breathless haste.

O'Hara instantly divined that something had happened, the more especially as he recognized in the new comer the face of Mick Hoolohan.

"For Heaven's sake, why this interruption?" he asked, as Hoolohan arrived heated and out of breath at the tomb.

"Hush, hush! Masther Charles," cried the poor fellow, gasping for breath, and lowering his voice to a whisper; "come aside for a minnit, I have somethin' to tell you."

Agitated and alarmed at his earnestness, O'Hara followed him anxiously a few paces, when he whispered a few words in his ear.

"My God! you do not say so!" exclaimed O'Hara, white as a ghost at the intelligence.

"Not a doubt of it, sir; I see the red coats of the villains as plain as the noonday."

"And going towards Glengarra, did you say?"

"Ay, within a thousand yards of it."

"But could you have been mistaken? How could he have been there?"

"Mavrone! I'd know his face among a million. 'Twas he, as sure as I'm a livin' man."

"Great heaven! and my sister is there alone."

"Betther than that, Masther Charles; immaydiately that I saw them, I flew like mad to the house an' warned Miss Milly. She towld me hurry to find you, an' that she would be all safe in the manetime."

"Enough, enough! not a moment is to be lost! Thank heaven! there is still hope. Can that horse of yours fly quickly!"

"The best in the stable, sir."

"Thirty, I think, you numbered them?"

"Somewhere about that; but half of 'em murdherin' cowards."

"'Tis well, then; there is yet time."

O'Hara returned, pale as death, but terribly resolute, to the astonished group around his father's grave.

"My friends," said he, "even a more sacred duty calls me hence without delay. I leave the dead to save the living. Remain, I pray you, to complete my father's obsequies. His heart, were he living, would follow me on my mission."

Before they could find speech for their surprise, he was gone from amongst them, and was mounted in the saddle. Another moment and he was riding away in mad career, striving in vain to equalize his pace with the winged fury of his thoughts.

Never did he draw bridle until his noble steed plunged into the depths of the Trooper's Glen.

The alarming clatter of horse's hoofs in the early morning aroused hundreds of half-armed men from their rude encampment in the groves, and brought them rushing in eager surprise round the horseman.

But immediately that they recognized him, they fell back respectfully, while, springing from the saddle, he hurried through the disordered group towards a thicket, where a rude green flag floated over the quarters of the chiefs.

The outlaw captain was already astir, indulging himself in the regalia of his new command, and surrounded by a little staff of fierce-looking peasants.

Without salute or preface, O'Hara briefly said: "The yeomanry have attacked Glengarra—my sister is in danger—we must instantly hasten to the rescue with a few of our choicest men."

"Miss O'Hara in danger!" cried the outlaw with kindling eyes. "Enough, sir; we will rescue her or die!"

In a few minutes, a body of about twenty of the best-armed and most determined of the insurgents was mustered, one half armed with such muskets as were at hand, and the rest with long pikes, in whose use the peasantry were particularly dexterous.

O'Hara took the command himself, and was supported by the outlaw captain, whose interest in the cause seemed scarcely less intense than O'Hara's. With hurried steps the compact little mass left the glen, and in less than half an hour caught sight of Glengarra.

His intimate knowledge of the place, as well as the notorious imbecility of the yeomanry corps, suggested to O'Hara an easy plan of attack. He advanced his men to the very edge of the plateau facing the main entrance to the house, under shelter of a deep copse. The silence at first led him to suppose that the villains had consummated their design and fled; but as they came nearer, he was at once reassured and alarmed to hear the noise of shouting and battering inside the house. It was, at least, evident that he was yet in time.

As he surmised, the yeomen, little expecting a surprise, had left all their horses outside the main entrance in charge of one of their body. He saw also at a glance that the heavy oaken door had been battered by blows and bullets, and he consequently conjectured that it had offered them a stout resistance. The noises within were ample evidence that the entire body of them were still engaged in overcoming other obstacles inside.

His resolution was instantly taken. Posting half of the men as a reserve, he dashed boldly at the front entrance with the other half.

The shock was irresistible. The sentinel fled in a panic; and the yeomen in the great entrance hall recoiled in confusion before the impetuous onslaught of the pikemen.

Half blinded by fury and resentment, O'Hara led the way up the broad staircase. A few of the redcoats fired their carbines at random, then joined their companions in a headlong flight anywhere out of reach of their pursuers.

With a wild cry of triumph, the insurgents mounted the steps, and spread panic among the yeomen on all sides.

Rushing through the corridors, O'Hara made furiously for his sister's chamber. It was at the end of a long gallery, approached from the main staircase by a narrow flight of stairs.

To his joy, he knew from the uproar and the redoubled blows on the panels that this chamber had not yet been forced. He even thought he could distinguish the cries for help raised by its brave mistress.

With a shout of mingled delight and vengeance, he cheered on his men to the attack on the gallery As they faced the narrow staircase, a voice he could not mistake was heard high above the din. It said: "Steady, men! fire!".

Scarcely was the order given, when five yoemen mustered at the head of the staircase delivered a murderous volley among the advancing assailants.

O'Hara felt the blinding smoke and smell of powder, and heard the bullets whistle past and above his head.

A shriek by his side told him the fire had not been without effect. He glanced hurriedly around, and saw the outlaw captain totter and fall heavily to the ground at his feet.

The insurgents paused and hesitated. O'Hara knew it was the crisis.

"Fire, men, and charge!" he shouted, furiously, himself bounding up the stairs through the smoke.

A volley from muskets and blunderbusses crashed through the gallery, and a cry of agony came from among the yeomen. Then the insurgents dashed up the steps with irresistible force, and the remnant of the yoemanry fled pell-mell through the passage.

But one remained immovable as a rock. With sword drawn, he stood unflinching before the advancing wave of steel; and as Charles O'Hara saw through the smoke that pale face and coal-black hair, he knew he was at last face to face with his enemy—met to decide once for all who was to be victor in their mysterious feud.

Their swords crossed with a loud crash.

"To the death!" shouted Inkston, with firmness.

"To the death be it!" shouted back his antagonist.

Instinctively, the men drew back to witness this strange duel. They were well matched swordsmen; but from the first, it was apparent that the dark-faced stranger struggled rather for honor than for life. Nevertheless, he parried skilfully every thrust of his opponent, until a pool of blood moistening the floor beneath his feet, he suddenly slipped heavily, and the sword dropped from his hand.

He was at O'Hara's mercy; but ere sword could be lifted or thought conceived, a report of a pistol shot came from behind, and, without a cry of agony, the wretched stranger fell prostrate on the ground.

O'Hara glanced fiercely round at the shooter. It was the Outlaw Captain, who had crawled, wounded and bleeding, from the spot where he had fallen, and now stood unsteadily a few paces off, the discharged pistol in his hand, grinning hideously at the accuracy of his aim.

Divided between relief and sorrow at this unexpected event, O'Hara had now little thought to spare for strangers. His first care was for his sister, whom he found utterly exhausted in her chamber. The struggle had been too much even for her dauntless heart.

A few minutes, however, served to restore her; and, womanly instinct still uppermost, she was hardly recovered when she hastened to assist those who had fallen in the affray.

Clinging to her brother's arm, she went out into the gallery. Most of the insurgents had dispersed in pursuit of the flying yeomen, and the wounded lay alone where they had fallen.

Involuntarily she shuddered and clung closer to her brother, as her eye fell on the ghastly scene.

Three bodies lay nearly together with the horrid marks of deadly combat on them. Almost at the chamber door, whither he had crept in a last effort, lay the chief of the outlaws, gasping painfully for breath. A few yards off, and close together, lay the other two victims—Inkston, placid, though paler than ever, and his faithful valet, James, with that quiet, silent face of his turned towards his master in death, and his lips more closely sealed than ever on the strange secret of his life. Inseparable while alive, there was something inexpressibly touching in their present deathly communion.

No sooner had Milly made her appearance in the gallery, than, with a supreme exertion, the outlaw murmured her name.

As she approached him, his dying face lit up with a glow of strange unearthly pleasure. She seemed to know intimately his feeling, for she bent down compassionately and imprinted a soft kiss on his rugged brow. His eyes gleamed in speechless gratitude; a quiver of delight passed through his frame; and then he fell back tranquilly. The fierce soul of the outlaw had passed away forever! Miss O'Hara could have wept over the corpse of him who to her alone in the world was generous and devoted; but the moment was not one for grief. She was recalled from her musing by her brother, who had passed on to where Inkston lay, and was engaged busily in examining him.

"Hush!" he whispered, suddenly, "he is still alive."

"Alive!" echoed Milly, hurrying to his side, with the quick instinct of benevolence.

"Yes; he is only insensible for the present. But he cannot live long. He is wounded somewhere in the region of the heart—his death can only be a question of hours."

"Ah! yes," she whispered softly, as she bent down to examine him. "The poor fellow has not long to live. Oh! Charlie, was it you did this?"

O'Hara pointed sadly to the outlaw's corse.

"Thank heaven it was not you!" she exclaimed, with a shudder. "But let us do what we can for the poor fellow; we must have him removed without delay."

"Yes, yes. I shall have them all removed immediately;" and he went in search of his men, who had by this time succeeded in capturing most of the frightened yeomanry.

Having taken all necessary precautions against another surprise, O'Hara set himself to removing the sad testimonies of the late struggle. Under Milly's supervision, Inkston's unconscious body was borne into an adjacent room, where his wound was stanched as best it might, and every restorative supplied with a careful hand.

It was wonderful—one other link in the chain of mystery that bound them together—with what anxious care brother and sister watched the feeble, flickering life of this unknown enemy, whose nameless feud had been the blight of their lives. Even yet that white face bore its strange fascination. Sorrow, rather than vice, was imprinted there. He was the victim, rather than the criminal. And he bore it all with such unearthly calmness—such unearthly silence.

CHAPTER XXVIII.

THE SILVER MASK.

THE anxious attentions of Milly O'Hara were not long without effect. By slow degrees, life began to return, and a feeble thrill to animate the veins of the sleeper.

Presently, the dark eyes opened, not flashing as of old, but wearily and heavily. As they met the anxious glances of his enemies, a thrill of pain seemed to convulse him. Then he put his hand to the wound in his side, and the whole story seemed to flash upon him.

For some moments he continued painfully musing, as if trying to collect his thoughts. The sight of all the arrangements for his comfort seemed to add to his embarrassment, as did the visible interest shown by both brother and sister, as they stood anxiously beside the bed.

On a sudden, his face contracted into an expression of resoluteness, such as, less painful to behold, used awe the companions of his college days, and he stretched out his thin white hand over the counterpane as a signal for them to approach nearer.

"Listen—and quickly," said he, in a voice little impaired by his debility. "I have much to say to you, and but a short time to say it."

O'Hara approached him kindly, and with an indefinable longing to hear the dread secret so long buried in that silent bosom.

At length, the mysterious power that had clouded all their lives was to be revealed, and the causes of their entire chain of sorrow were to be laid bare!

"Perhaps you had better not exert yourself by speaking now," he whispered, gently; "some other time."

"Some other time!" echoed the dying man, with the faint mockery of a smile. "There is no other time for me. It is because I know my time is drawing to a close that I speak at all."

"You would tell, then, of the hidden motive you had in pursuing us with such incessant vengeance."

"Yes, yes, I would tell you all—the knowledge can hurt no one now. All, all of us are gone. But listen, and do not interrupt me, I have not much strength left, and the hand of death is upon me already."

With eager attention, Charles O'Hara and his sister listened to the strange recital, while the dying man, pausing for a few moments to allay the pain and collect his resolution, began thus:—

"Nineteen years ago, in the Bois de Clamart, near Paris, there was a duel one bright May morning. A nobleman—one of the best blood of Corsica—had challenged a court favorite, and the nobleman fell mortally wounded. Dying there under the tall trees, he raised the sword dripping with his blood, and he made his boy —little more than a child then—swear before heaven on that sword that he would wipe out the disgrace of his house in blood or die in the attempt. He died, and the boy has kept the oath. That nobleman was my father; that boy was myself."

"Heavens!—and his murderer!"

"Ay, his murderer, and worse than murderer, was your father!"

O'Hara and his sister were struck dumb with horror

and dismay. Already the mystery of their lives was unwinding itself with terrible distinctness.

"Worse than murderer, I say," continued the dying man, in a harsh whisper, "because the murderer of his honor—the betrayer of *his* wife and *my* mother. You now know the secret of my life."

Miss O'Hara had swooned in her brother's arms. That black-haired stranger was terrible to behold, as he hissed out the burning words of shame.

Then he became calm again as he proceeded :—

"The history of the wrong is brief, and I have but little time to tell it. My father, Giuseppe de Marsini, Count of Villeggia, was old, and but newly come to court. A rude Corsican noble, he was little versed in the intrigues of the palace. Your father, young, handsome, and courtly, was a favorite of the monarch, and was one of the most profligate of his dissolute court. My mother, much younger than her husband, was praised for her beauty until her poor head was turned by the gaudy glare and pomp she saw around her. Why follow out a story that scorches my heart in the telling? She—poor frail angel!—she was ruined; our house—ay, a house ennobled by centuries—was disgraced, and the Bois de Clamart saw our cup of bitterness filled to overflowing."

"Oh! but he atoned for it well," cried O'Hara, into whose heart this revelation sank like a burning coal. "Now I know why he left Paris, and why he pined away his life in misery. Oh! if you could but have seen him as I have seen him, you would have pardoned him."

"Pardoned him!" interrupted the other, his eyes blazing with unhealthy light. "In the Corsican's vocabulary there is no such word as *pardon*. Pardoned him! Blood alone could wipe out such an injury.

Scarcely two months after his death, I stood by the death-bed of my mother. Shame and sorrow broke her heart, and with her dying breath she consecrated the *vendetta* which I had made the object of my life."

O'Hara shuddered.

"Yes, and on her coffin I renewed my oath, and swore that life alone should terminate my vengeance. Let the sequel show how I have kept my pledge!"

He smiled ghastlily, and then paused wearily for breath ere he resumed:—

"From the morning of the duel, your father was never seen again at the French court. I doubt not he felt deeply the ruin he had wrought."

"Oh! believe he did!" cried Miss O'Hara, who was again eagerly listening. "He has never been seen to smile."

"No matter," muttered the dying man, with a feeble wave of the hand, "no matter; not all the sighs and groans of Christendom conbined could bend my purpose, or make atonement for a ruined home and dishonored name.

"But I delay, and my strength is going fast. I have said that your father disappeared from Paris. I was at the time too young to trace his whereabouts; but there was a Corsican servant in our family, Giovanni Suglino, who loved my father well, and joined me in the oath to avenge his quarrel. For nineteen years that man has never left my side, until this very morning he fell dead at my feet."

"James?"

"Yes. Like a true friend he has attended me even in death. Well, he ascertained the place of refuge of your father, and before I was yet fifteen years of age, I left my lonely Corsican home for ever, to enter on the crusade against my enemy. I had riches enough; but they were as nothing to me. Life had but one object, one hope, one desire—revenge!

"I renounced my name, and disposed of all that remained to our house. I thought if ever I should return to Corsica, I should only return to die. I parted, therefore, with every association of country and friends, and set out for England, where for eight long years I prepared myself for vengeance. I determined it should be no mean question of life for life, but years of agony, growing more and more bitter until it should become unendurable. Oh! often and often, in my morbid fits of thought, I weaved for my enemy in fancy the lengthening chain of torture, by which I should by slow degrees extinguish his every hope, embitter his every thought, and crush him down into his grave with a broken heart. Ay, I even fancied myself standing over that grave, and seeing an outraged mother pursue him into his dark eternity with vengeance. For such is a Corsican's hate!"

"Oh! this is too horrible!" cried Miss O'Hara, white as a ghost.

"Spare it to us," said her brother. "Heaven knows you have had your revenge. We know the rest"——

"Nay," cried the dying man, altering his fierce tone to one of half entreaty. "There are stranger things still to follow. I shall not trouble you long, and, perchance, you may wish to hear what I have to say."

He stopped again to recover some little energy, and then proceeded:—

"When I found that my enemy had settled down in Ireland, I also discovered that he had children, whom he loved more than his life. Here was at once the opportunity above all others I had craved—an opportunity, at the same time, of extirpating the whole hated race, and of making his punishment the more intolerable by stabbing him through his own kindred. You may well shudder; but what seems so terrible to you wore *then* for me the seductive guise of honor and duty.

"Well, having learned of your entry into Trinity College, I formed the scheme that will end in merited death a few moments hence. I crossed over to Ireland, and entered college with you under the name of Inkston. What followed there I need not repeat. Enough to say, that my success more than realized my anticipations. You were gay, thoughtless, warm-hearted. I was what the world called gifted, and had little difficulty in winding myself into your confidence. But now began the retribution for my deceit. I succeeded in becoming your friend: *but I succeeded too well!*"

"Too well?"

"Yes, too well. I became your friend that I might be more effectually your enemy. Instead of that I only added myself to the number of my foes. Henceforth, I hated myself more for my treachery than I hated you for the name you bore"——

"Heavens! you do not mean it?"

"Mean it!—I am already on the brink of the grave—there is no longer need of falsehood. Yes, I found I had misappreciated myself. Up to the time I knew you, I knew no one else in the world but my vengeance and Suglino. My mind was filled with thoughts of an outraged mother, of a bleeding father, of a dishonored name. Nothing holy or pure ever entered into my thoughts. I was, in fact, the Corsican, and lived only for my revenge. I forgot that I was also the *man*, or, at any rate, I fancied that every soft emotion of my heart was dried up. I was mistaken. Your generous affection called into life a thousand powerful passions I had never dreamt of. They raged within my breast—they ranged themselves opposite me and my vengeance—and, from that moment, I was at deadly war against the world. I stood alone with the one dark object of my life, and everything deserted me but misery and unhappiness."

A powerful change had come over his listeners. Miss O'Hara was weeping silently, while Charles followed this mysterious being through the new phase of his wretched life with a feeling of engrossing interest that almost overpowered him.

The dying man himself spoke in broken accents, as if in unspeakable pain.

"What I suffered," he continued, "during those four weary years, may heaven take into account in mitigation of my crime! It matters not now to tell of it, since it is past for ever. Many and many a time I would have slain myself rather than meet your open, generous glance."

"Alas! often, often, I have noticed those dark shadows of unhappiness creep over your face, and have wondered what they were."

"There were shadows of the deadly strife within my breast. They escaped betimes from their gloomy prison-house. But, still," he cried, with a return of the old vehemence—" still I never faltered in my purpose, or lost sight of my vengeance. I might die of a broken heart—I hoped for nothing more—but my oath—the oath registered by my mother's death-bed—*that* should be accomplished, no matter what the issue. Accordingly, having learned your father's sentiments, I engaged you, as you know, in the project I knew to be most repugnant to his feelings—that namely of revolution. Even then, I had planned your breach with your father, which subsequent events so materially promoted. I ministered, too, to my revenge, by reflecting on your college successes: but that was, I confess, more to oppose additional resistance to the clamorous voice of conscience, than any real regret of my ill-fortune. Well, you are aware of how I got you pledged to the revolutionary embassy. To promote my plans, as well as (as I then thought) to enkindle my revenge anew, I accepted your invitation to visit Glengarra "——

"Yes, yes—spare yourself the pain of going farther," cried O'Hara, utterly lost between pity and amazement. "We know the rest too well."

"Nay, you know but half," said the dying man, with a deathly smile. "The other half is stranger still. I come to Glengarra in the hope that, there, at least, in the presence of my enemy, I should rid myself of my better self, and return without obstacle to my projects of revenge. Alas! I was but plunging into a more fiery furnace! Miss O'Hara, you will bear with what I say now, for, thank heaven! it shall never be in my power to pain you again. From the first moment I saw you, a new and more terrible passion rose up to complete my torture. Forgive me if I call it love—it *was* love—love too pure and holy to find resting-place in my foul breast. I had yet a strong will—God alone knows how strong—and I wrestled with my passion until I almost strangled myself. I knew how hopeless, how criminal it was—but it was still beyond the power of my will to overcome.

"In a fatal moment—when my heart was bruised and torn by hostile passions—I yielded to a fiendish impulse. I determined to unite my love with my revenge, and to retaliate on my enemy for a mother's ruin by the betrayal of his darling daughter."

So inured had she become to horrors, the fair girl merely raised her eyes to heaven in tearful thanksgiving

"I do not ask your pardon, Miss O'Hara," continued

he, growing fainter and fainter; "I am still your enemy until death, and could not accept of your forgiveness, did you even offer it. Yet I can adore the divine Providence that has shielded you—I can even thank it. But enough of that. I have but little time left.

"You know how the election favored my project, and know also now how well I succeeded in blighting your home, and breaking your father's heart. If my own was not broken also, all joy and hope had forsaken it forever. I only fed on my revenge and on my guilty passion. But, through all, my sacred oath of vengeance was being surely accomplished. You had left your father's house, and nothing seemed to stand between me and my unholy love.

"Well, I was baffled, and I was glad of it. Before I left Glengarra, however, I told your father who I was. What passed at that interview, I have not the heart to tell. I knew that my vengeance—my house's honor—was satisfied, and that the old man's heart was broken. Vengeance had long lost its charms for me, and success made me only more miserable. My father's death—my mother's ruin—were still present to my mind, and made my revenge as much a solemn duty as ever; but I hated myself for the blight my wretched existence scattered all around it.

"For some time after leaving Glengarra, I wandered about the neighborhood, watching for a time when I might satiate both love and hatred at once. No opportunity came till I heard your father was dying. Then I watched with redoubled vigilance, until I learned that you had come home to his death-bed. I did more—I learned that the insurrection was planned, and that you were to be its leader in this quarter. Your father's death at the same time suggested to me one last desperate effort to carry off the object of my passion.

"Last night I repaired to Clonmel, and by an enormous bribe I procured from Captain Crofts the command of his troop of yeomanry for the night, that my success might be the more crushing by having the sanction of the law. I do not wonder that you shudder at my cold-blooded schemes—but think that I was a savage by instinct—a savage, alone and vengeful in a cold-hearted world—and think, also, that any good that was in me served only to aggravate my misery.

"Little remains to be told. I watched my opportunity the live-long night in yonder wood. Though success seemed to be within my grasp, I knew that I was approaching my end, and I hurried to meet it, heaven knows how gladly! You know the rest. Immediately that the funeral started I pounced upon what I thought was my defenceless prey. I took no precaution, and thought none necessary. I found we were betrayed, and that the doors offered a stubborn resistance. We got through them, however, and my victim was already within reach when—when my hour struck, and heaven's vengeance seized upon me!"

As he finished, Giuseppe de Marsini leaned back, as if sick even to death, while his dark eyes seemed searching, searching into the future.

Charles O'Hara and his sister were speechless with grief and a growing feeling of pity for this wretched child of destiny. He looked hardly less handsome than ever, lying there within sight of the grave, his jetty black hair clustering round the broad, white brow, and the warm olive-tinge of the south paling into the sickly shadow of death. Surely he was not all bad!

Suddenly he spoke again.

"I have said," he whispered, feebly, "that I am your enemy till death—I have sworn it, and it must be so—but *after* death, when I am cold forever, and cannot hurt you any more, I think—yes, I *know* it would soothe me if—if you could both stand over my grave, and pity me. I ask nothing else."

Miss O'Hara fell on her knees by the bedside in a torrent of tears. O'Hara, almost choked with emotion, took the dying man's hand fervently.

"Nay, nay," he cried, withdrawing the cold hand in a last effort, "not that—I do not deserve it. But—but I feel—I know you will pity me, both of you. And I—I shall love you—I shall pray for you—when there is no longer need for hating you."

The watchers by the bedside were blinded by their tears.

"And now," said the dying man, stretching his wan hand with difficulty to his neck, and holding to his lips those same miniatures he had embraced so often before —"now father! mother! I have kept my oath! You are avenged—and—and—so—is—heaven!"

The voice died away—the head fell heavily back. When Charles O'Hara bent down to that white face, Giuseppe de Marsini was dead!

The Silver Mask was raised, and the soul it covered was gone to another world.

CHAPTER XXIX.

CLOUDLAND FADING.

TIME was too pressing to allow Charles O'Hara many moments' meditation over the fate of his strange friend-enemy. It was already close upon the time when the Dublin envoy was expected with the final orders for the march of the insurrectionary army. He feared, besides, that some of the escaped yeomanry would not be long in bringing the military force at Clonmel upon them, and he hesitated to provoke any other collision that might interfere with the plans of the Revolutionary Directory.

He, therefore, freely unburdened himself to his sister, whose courageous spirit, now steeled to scenes of horror and danger, was prepared for almost any calamity.

"Not a moment is to be lost, Milly," he said, pressing her fondly in his arms. "Our fellows will be on the march directly, and it is worse than useless to remain longer here."

"What! then we must abandon Glengarra?"

"Yes, yes, child, for the present. Please God, we shall return to it in happier times."

"I hope so," she murmured, as a tear stole down her cheek, in spite of all her fortitude.

"Nay, Milly, you are not used to be so faint-hearted."

"Faint-hearted, Charlie!—oh! how can you say so, when you see me so calm and firm in the midst of all those terrible scenes."

"True, true, darling," he cried, kissing her pale

cheek tenderly. "You are more than brave. The strongest heart would sicken at all you have endured within the last two days. But what *can* I do now? It would be criminal to delay"——

"Then why not go?"

"But you, dearest Milly—I could not leave you alone here"——

"Why—can I not go with you?"

"But think of the danger—the uncertainty. You could never stand such scenes as we are entering on."

"Far better see them than be thinking of them," said she, firmly; then clasping him fondly round the neck, "Take me with you, Charlie," she cried, eagerly; "I will not be in your way, and it would kill me to be left thus alone. Believe me, I am now brave enough to face the worst."

"Then be it so, dearest sister," he cried, kissing her over and over again. "You shall come with me. We will be blessed all the more for your presence. But, stay—you must bring one thing at least with you."

He rushed from the room, and in a few moments returned with an open parchment in his hand.

"It is just as I expected, dearest Milly," he cried joyfully, glancing over the parchment. "Poor father made his will before his reconciliation with me, and he left the entire property to you"——

"To me!"

"Yes, dear, and it's the most fortunate thing in the world"——

"Fortunate!"

"Of course it is. Whatever happens now, they cannot deprive you of the property, since it is solely and entirely yours. So, if all does not go well with us, or if anything should happen me, they cannot lay a finger on your estate."

"Charlie! do not speak of that!"

"Why not, Milly? You must preserve this will carefully. But time flies. We have yet to bury those poor fellows."

He hastened in search of his men, whom he found collected sadly round a couch on which was placed the corpse of the Outlaw Chief. There was something mournful and touching in the grief of those rude hearts for him whose name had been so often the symbol of terror throughout the wide district swayed by his arbitrary ukase.

With difficulty O'Hara mustered them together in the Hall, when a horseman dashed up the avenue, and, leaping hastily from his foaming steed, was in the hall and grasping O'Hara's hand, before the latter recognized him as Jack Colthurst!

"In heaven's name!" cried O'Hara, staring at him in amazement, "in heaven's name can it be you?"

"Hush, hush! I'll tell you all immediately," replied Colthurst, still gasping for breath. "First tell me, has the insurrection broken out here?"

"Of course it has; but what"——

"My God! Has any harm been done?"

"How?"

"Is it known the rebellion is begun?"

"Well, no—as yet we've only had a brush with the yeomen."

"Bravo! I'm glad of that."

"But, in heaven's name, what do you mean? Where have you come from? What's up?"

"It's *all* up, man," cried Colthurst, fanning his perspiring brow.

"What's all up? You speak in riddles."

"The revolution's all up, man. Disperse your men instanter."

"For goodness' sake, speak calmly, Jack."

"Calmly! By my word, a man can't be very calm who's ridden like a mad man through the country all night long."

"Where, then, have you come from?"

"From Dublin, to be sure. The revolution was planned to commence last night; but—the usual story—somebody sold the pass—all the leaders were arrested or forced to fly from Dublin, and all they could do was to send emissaries in hot haste to every part of the country to recall the orders for a rising. I was sent to your district, and here I am, just in the nick of time, after the most infernal night's run I ever had in the entire course of my life."

"Then the rising is over?"

"I hope so. Let you, at any rate, disperse your men without a moment's delay. Let every one return home as if nothing had happened."

Without delay O'Hara communicated the order to one of his men, who immediately galloped off to the encampment at the Trooper's Glen.

"But tell me, Jack," he asked, as Colthurst flung himself into a chair in utter exhaustion, "what brought you to Dublin? Where is Lucy? Why did you leave Paris?"

"Hand me that wine-jug beyond there, or I'll die of drought," cried the captain, helping himself to an ample measure of the beverage. "Ha! *mavrone*, that's something after a drive of a hundred miles. What's that you were asking me, Charlie? Oh!—why I left Paris? You hadn't gone a full week when poor Hoche took sick and died."

"Died!"

"Ay, just at the moment the world wanted him most. When he died I had no longer any business in Paris"

"Well, and Lucy—what of her?"

"She was terribly worn out, poor child! Ever since you left, she was never the same."

"Well, well—and where is she now?"

"Mercy! how you *do* gallop! She is in Dublin, of course. We returned only yesterday, and I had hardly eaten my dinner after the voyage, when this unfortunate affair of the insurrection occurred, and, as there was no one else left to go, I was packed off to Tipperary to stop the rising."

"I'm perfectly bewildered by all that's happening," cried O'Hara. "I fancy the world is going topsy-turvy."

"All for the best, old boy—all for the best. But now for *my* round of questions—How is Milly? Has the old gentleman weathered his fit? How are you all getting on at Glengarra?"

It was a sad and pregnant tale—that of the last two days of Glengarra; and as they sat all three round the fire in the great dining-room, and talked over the crowding incidents of the story, Charles O'Hara was half inclined to doubt whether it had not been all some oppressive nightmare, so vivid was it with horrors.

But the emblems of mourning, and the white dead face were yet within sight, to remind him of its bitter reality.

What was to be done now? was the question that occurred to them after exchanging their mutual confidences.

"I cannot certainly remain," said O'Hara, "I must leave the country. This unfortunate shooting affray can never be satisfactorily explained."

"And it appears I'm compromised by those Dublin arrests," said Colthurst, "so the less time we lose about our flight the better."

"Then I shall certainly go with you," cried Miss O'Hara; "I could never endure remaining here by myself."

"But before we do anything," added O'Hara, "I have one duty to perform. Poor Inkston and the others remain unburied. We must first see to their decent interment."

"Oh! yes," cried his sister, "and I should wish the poor fellow were laid beside dear papa. They will be at peace together in death."

While they spoke, Mick Hoolohan burst into the room with an agitated face, and summoned them to the window overlooking the front of the house.

With a cry of alarm, Miss O'Hara sank fainting into her brother's arms. The entire avenue was swarming with an advancing body of infantry and cavalry, whose bright arms and accoutrements shone dazzlingly in the sunlight. Detached parties were scouring the park on all sides, and marching to the rear of the house to intercept the flight of the inmates.

Freed from all their late dangers, it seemed as if O'Hara and Colthurst were now at last in the very arms of death. Agreeably to instructions, the little body of insurgents had dispersed, and it would be worse than madness for themselves alone to attempt any resistance against such a force as now surrounded them on all sides. But on all sides, equally, death seemed to encompass them.

"If they take us alive," said Colthurst, coolly, "they'll surely hang us; so there's little choice. We'll fight it out with the fellows."

"Decidedly," cried O'Hara, laying his sister gently on a sofa, kissing her white lips and then springing back resolutely to the window. "Heaven be our judge; 'tis in a good cause we die!"

"Hallo! what's that?" exclaimed Colthurst, suddenly, scanning the advancing soldiers carefully. "Eh? 'Tis Crabshawe, for a million!"

The main body of the military had halted in front of the house, and a horseman, dressed as a civilian, advanced out of the ranks, waving a white handkerchief as a token of truce. As he came nearer, there could be no mistake about him. It was the redoubtable Lord Crabshawe himself.

He advanced timidly at first—then, seeing no sign of resistance, approached the main entrance boldly. In another moment he was face to face with Charles O'Hara and his old rival, Captain Colthurst.

His lordship looked better than ever, and seemed to be quite happy in contrast with his old mumbling crotchety self.

"Aw, Mr. O'Hara—Captain Colthurst—delighted to see you—yawz," he cried, raising his hat with a clumsy sort of cordiality. "You see I pay you this visit for your own benefit. Yawz, indeed, I assure you."

"Faith, then, my lord, you take a mighty queer way of showing it," said Colthurst, pointing jocosely to the long line of military on the area outside.

"Well, well," continued his lordship, fishing as usual for his sentences in some remote corner of the room—"the fact is, I want to talk to you. Perhaps you don't know I've got married"——

"Oh! indeed, my lord?"

"Yawz, an excellent creature—quite an angel. Well, you see she wants me to—to settle down, you know; so I got appointed lord lieutenant of Tipperary, and returned from London yesterday"——

"Well, my lord?" said O'Hara, wondering what in the world all this had to do with his present mission.

"Well, you see, my wife—a beautiful creature, I

assure you—she—at least I—that is, we're a quiet sort of people, and don't want any fighting or quarrelling, or anything of that sort. And, besides, I like you all very much—especially Miss Milly—I do, indeed, very much "——

"Well, my lord?"

"Well, you see, I heard of this scrape you've got into, and I know all about it; and I tell you candidly I don't half like seeing fine fellows like you hung, or that sort of thing; and, in fact, I've come to offer you the king's pardon for everything that has occurred, and to ask you to settle down among us like jolly good fellows."

Lord Crabshawe was a happy man that night, as he sat by Milly O'Hara's side, and received her burning thanks for his unpretentious goodness. They were all happy, for the clouds were lifting gently, and the bright summer sky of hope and happiness was already glittering through the mists of sadness.

CHAPTER XXX.

AT LAST!

THE fresh light of an early autumn morning streams in through the windows and tips the humble altar with gold. The white-headed priest is beaming with gentle smiles, as he receives a double marriage *cortege*. Two happy couples stand together before the altar in the golden light. And Lord Crabshawe is there to give away Milly O'Hara; and Father Mat Ryan is there to render up Lucy Colthurst to the husband of her choice. And heaven's own benediction poured in on them with the sunlight, and enveloped them in its blessed rays.

For peace had come at last, and their hearts were full of happiness.

* * * * * * * *

Five years rolled away: and Glengarra was bright once more. The hoary old mansion, no longer deserted, rang with the happy mirth that had held court there long ago; the park was gay with the merry laughter of children; the flowers were blooming in the gardens; the deer were sporting in the woods; the grand old cry of fox and hound once again woke the echoes of the hills. Many a time, in the long winter nights, the vast dining-room was ablaze with lights; and Charles O'Hara did the honors with lordly grace; and his sweet bride scattered joy and happiness around her. Then Colthurst would set the table in a roar with his brimming humor; and Lord Crabshawe would laugh a brave, honest laugh, and think proudly of the old sad times; while Milly—enchanting Milly—now blossoming into all the charms of the matron, would say cheerily that Glengarra was itself again.

And often, too, when the dear family circle would gather round the hearth in the flickering light, their thoughts would wander away to those twin graves in the churchyard beyond, where, side by side, slept Giuseppe de Marsini and his enemy in life. And then a whispered prayer would go up into the night, and a mute thanksgiving to Him who had ordered all things so well.

www.ingramcontent.com/pod-product-compliance
Lightning Source LLC
Chambersburg PA
CBHW031353230426
43670CB00006B/523